Allyn
and
Bacon

*Research
Navigator Guide*

Sociology

Joe Jacoby
Bowling Green State University

Linda R. Barr
University of the Virgin Islands

PEARSON

Boston | New York | San Francisco
Mexico City | Montreal | Toronto | London | Madrid | Munich | Paris
Hong Kong | Singapore | Tokyo | Cape Town | Sydney

ISBN   0-205-40827-3

Printed in the United States of America

10 9 8 7 6 5 4 3 2 1   08 07 06 05 04 03

Contents

Introduction

Your professor assigns a research paper or group report that's due in two weeks—and you need to make sure you have up-to-date, credible information. Where do you begin? Today, the easiest answer is the Internet—because it can be so convenient and there is so much information out there. But therein lies part of the problem. How do you know if the information is reliable and from a trustworthy source?

Research Navigator Guide: Sociology is designed to help you select and evaluate research from the Web to help you find the best and most credible information you can. Throughout this guide, you'll find:

- **A Quick Guide to Research Navigator.** All you need to know to get started with Research Navigator™, a research database that gives you immediate access to hundreds of scholarly journals and other popular publications, such as *Scientific American, U.S. News & World Report,* and many others.
- **A practical and to-the-point discussion of search engines.** Find out which search engines are likely to get you the information you want and how to phrase your searches for the most effective results.
- **Detailed information on evaluating online sources.** Locate credible information on the Web and get tips for thinking critically about Web sites.
- **Citation guidelines for Web resources.** Learn the proper citation guidelines for Web sites, email messages, listservs, and more.
- **Web activities for Sociology.** Explore the various ways you can use the Web in your courses through these online exercises.
- **Web links for Sociology.** Begin your Web research with the discipline-specific sources listed in this section. Also included is information about Web resources offered by Allyn & Bacon—these sites are designed to give you an extra boost in your Abnormal Psychology courses.

So before running straight to your browser, take the time to read through this copy of *Research Navigator Guide: Sociology* and use it as a reference for all of your Web research needs.

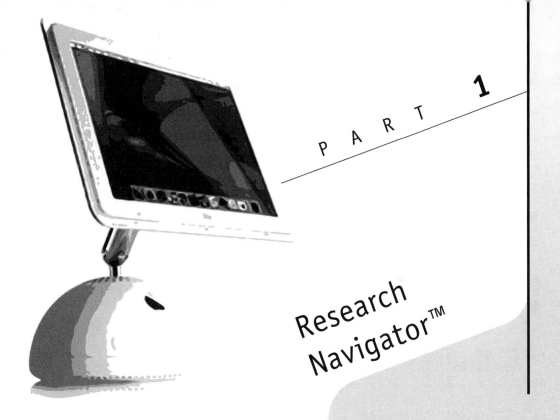

Research
Navigator™

What Is Research Navigator™?

Research Navigator™ is the easiest way for you to start a research assignment or research paper. Complete with extensive help on the research process and three exclusive databases of credible and reliable source material (including EBSCO's ContentSelect™ Academic Journal and Abstract Database, *New York Times* Search by Subject Archive, and Link Library), Research Navigator™ helps you quickly and efficiently make the most of your research time.

Research Navigator™ includes three databases of dependable source material to get your research process started:

1. EBSCO's ContentSelect™ Academic Journal and Abstract Database, organized by subject, contains 50–100 of the leading academic journals per discipline. Instructors and students can search the online journals by keyword, topic, or multiple topics. Articles include abstract and citation information and can be cut, pasted, emailed, or saved for later use.
2. The *New York Times* Search by Subject Archive is organized by academic subject and searchable by keyword, or multiple keywords. Instructors and students can view full-text articles from the world's leading journalists from *The New York Times*. The *New York Times*

Search by Subject Archive is available exclusively to instructors and students through Research Navigator™.

3. Link Library, organized by subject, offers editorially selected "Best of the Web" sites. Link libraries are continually scanned and kept up to date, providing the most relevant and accurate links for research assignments.

In addition, Research Navigator™ includes extensive online content detailing the steps in the research process including:

- Starting the Research Process
- Finding and Evaluating Sources
- Citing Sources
- Internet Research
- Using your Library
- Starting to Write

Registering with Research Navigator™

http://www.researchnavigator.com

Research Navigator™ is simple to use and easy to navigate. The goal of Research Navigator™ is to help you complete research assignments or research papers quickly and efficiently. The site is organized around the following tabs:

- Home
- Research Process
- Finding Sources
- Using Your Library

In order to begin using Research Navigator™, you must first register using the personal access code that appears in the front cover of this book.

To Register:

4. Go to **http://www.researchnavigator.com**
5. Click "Register" under "New Users" on the left side of the screen.
6. Enter the access code exactly as it appears on the inside front cover of this book. (Note: Access codes can only be used once to complete one registration. If you purchased a used guide, the access code may not work. Please go to **www.researchnavigator.com** for information on how to obtain a new access code.)
7. Follow the instructions on screen to complete your registration—you may click the Help button at any time if you are unsure how to respond.
8. Once you have successfully completed registration, write down the Login Name and Password you just created and keep it in a safe place.

You will need to enter it each time you want to revisit Research Navigator™.

9. Once you register, you have access to all the resources in Research Navigator™ for twelve months.

Getting Started

From the Research Navigator™ homepage, you have easy access to all of the site's main features, including a quick route to the three exclusive databases of source content that will be discussed in greater detail on the following pages. If you are new to the research process, you may want to start by clicking the *Research Process* tab, located in the upper right hand section of the page. Here you will find extensive help on all aspects of the research process, including:

- Introduction to the Research Paper
- Gathering Data
- Searching the Internet
- Evaluating Sources
- Organizing Ideas
- Writing Notes
- Drafting the Paper
- Academic Citation Styles (MLA, APA, CME, and more)
- Blending Reference Material into Your Writing
- Practicing Academic Integrity
- Revising
- Proofreading
- Editing the Final Draft

For those of you who are already familiar with the research process, you already know that the first step in completing a research assignment or research paper is to select a topic. (In some cases, your instructor may assign you a topic.) According to James D. Lester in *Writing Research Papers,* choosing a topic for the research paper can be easy (any topic will serve) yet very complicated (an informed choice is critical). He suggests selecting a person, a person's work, or a specific issue to study—President George W. Bush, John Steinbeck's *Of Mice and Men,* or learned dexterity with Nintendo games. Try to select a topic that will meet three demands.

1. It must examine a significant issue.
2. It must address a knowledgeable reader and carry that reader to another level of knowledge.
3. It must have a serious purpose, one that demands analysis of the issues, argues from a position, and explains complex details.

You can find more tips from Lester in the *Research Process* section of Research Navigator™.

Research Navigator™ simplifies your research efforts by giving you a convenient launching pad for gathering data on your topic. The site has aggregated three distinct types of source material commonly used in research assignments: academic journals (ContentSelect™); newspaper articles (*New York Times*) and world wide Web sites (Link Library).

EBSCO's ContentSelect Academic Journal and Abstract Database

EBSCO's ContentSelect Academic Journal and Abstract Database contains scholarly, peer-reviewed journals (like the *Journal of Clinical Psychology* or the *Journal of Anthropology*). A scholarly journal is an edited collection of articles written by various authors and is published several times per year. All the issues published in one calendar year comprise a volume of that journal. For example, the *American Sociological Review* published volume 65 in the year 2000. This official journal of the American Sociological Association is published six times a year, so issues 1–6 in volume 65 are the individual issues for that year. Each issue contains between 4 and 8 articles written by a variety of authors. Additionally, journal issues may contain letters from the editor, book reviews, and comments from authors. Each issue of a journal does not necessarily revolve around a common theme. In fact, most issues contain articles on many different topics.

Scholarly journals, are similar to magazines in that they are published several times per year and contain a variety of articles in each issue, however, they are NOT magazines. What sets them apart from popular magazines like *Newsweek* or *Science News* is that the content of each issue is peer-reviewed. This means that each journal has, in addition to an editor and editorial staff, a pool of reviewers. Rather than a staff of writers who write something on assignment, journals accept submissions from academic researchers all over the world. The editor relies on these peer reviewers both to evaluate the articles, which are submitted, and to decide if they should be accepted for publication. These published articles provide you with a specialized knowledge and information about your research topic. Academic journal articles adhere to strict scientific guidelines for methodology and theoretical grounding. The information obtained in these individual articles is more scientific than information you would find in a popular magazine, newspaper article, or on a Web page.

Using ContentSelect

Searching for articles in ContentSelect is easy! Here are some instructions and search tips to help you find articles for your research paper.

Research Navigator Guide: Sociology

Step 1: **Select an academic subject and topic area.** When you first enter the ContentSelect Research Database, you will see a list of disciplines. To search within a single academic subject, click the name of that subject. In order to search in more than one academic subject, hold down the alt or command key. In the space below where all the subjects are listed, you must enter a topic area. For example if you choose Psychology as an academic subject you might enter "Freud" as a topic area.

Step 2: Click the **GO** button to start your search.

Step 3: **Basic Search.** By clicking **GO** you will be brought to the *Basic Search* tab. Basic Search lets you search for articles using a variety of methods. You can select from: Standard Search, All Words, Any Words, or Exact Phrase. For more information on these options, click the **<u>Search Tips</u>** link at any time!

Step 4: After you have selected your method Click **Search.**

Some ways to improve your search:

Tip 1: **Using AND, OR, and NOT** to help you search. In Standard Search, you can use AND, OR and NOT to create a very broad or very narrow search:

- **AND** searches for articles containing all of the words. For example, typing **education AND technology** will search for articles that contain **both** education AND technology.
- **OR** searches for articles that contains at least one of the terms. For example, searching for **education OR technology** will find articles that contain either education OR technology.
- **NOT** excludes words so that the articles will not include the word that follows "NOT." For example, searching for **education NOT technology** will find articles that contain the term education but NOT the term technology.

Tip 2: **Using All Words.** When you select the "All Words" option, you do not need to use the word AND—you will automatically search for articles that only contain all of the words. The order of the search words entered in does not matter. For example, typing **education technology** will search for articles that contain **both** education AND technology.

Tip 3: **Using Any Words.** After selecting the "Any Words" option, type words, a phrase, or a sentence in the window. ContentSelect will search for articles that contain any of the terms you typed (but will not search for words such as **in** and **the**). For example, type **rising medical costs in the United States** to find articles that contain *rising, medical, costs, United,* or *States.* To limit your search to find articles that contain exact terms, use *quotation marks*—for example, typing "United States" will only search for articles containing "United States."

Tip 4: **Using Exact Phrase.** Select this option to find articles containing an exact phrase. ContentSelect will search for articles that include all the words you entered, exactly as you entered them. For example, type **rising medical costs in the United States** to find articles that contain the exact phrase "rising medical costs in the United States."

Search by Article Number

Each and every article in EBSCO's ContentSelect Academic Journal and Abstract Database is assigned its own unique article number. In some instances, you may know the exact article number for the journal article you want to retrieve. Perhaps you noted it during a prior research session on Research Navigator™. Such article numbers might also be found on the companion web site for your text, or in the text itself.

To retrieve a specific article, simply type that article number in the "Search by Article Number" field and click the **GO** button.

Advanced Search

The following tips will help you with an Advanced Search.

Step 1: To switch to an **Advanced Search**, from the Basic Search click the *AdvancedSearch* tab on the navigation bar, just under the EBSCO Host logo. The *AdvancedSearch* tab helps you focus your search using keyword searching, search history and limiters.

Step 2: Type the words you want to search for in the **Find** field.

Step 3: Click on **Field Codes** to see a list of available field codes for limiting your search. For example: AU-Author, will limit your search to an author. Enter one of these two-letter field codes before your search term. For example, if you enter AU-Smith, this will limit your results to SMITH in the Author field. For more information on field codes, click **Search Tips**.

Step 4: After you have added the appropriate Field Code to your topic, click **Search.**

Some ways to improve your search:

Tip 1: You can enter additional search terms in the **Find** field, and remember to use *and, or,* and *not* to connect multiple search terms (see Tip 1 under Basic Search for information on *and, or,* and *not*).

Tip 2: With Advanced Searches you can also use **Limiters** and **Expanders** to refine your search. For more information on Limiters and Expanders, click **Search Tips**.

The *New York Times* Search by Subject Archive

Newspapers, also known as periodicals because they are issued in periodic installments (e.g. daily, weekly, or monthly), provide contemporary information. Information in periodicals—journals, magazines, and newspapers—may be useful, or even critical, when you are ready to focus in on specific aspects of your topic, or to find more up-to-date information.

There are some significant differences between newspaper articles and journal articles, and you should consider the level of scholarship that is most appropriate for your research. Popular or controversial topics may not be well covered in journals, even though coverage in newspapers and "general interest" magazines like *Newsweek* and *Science* for that same topic may be extensive.

Research Navigator™ gives you access to a one-year, "search by subject" archive of articles from one of the world's leading newspapers—*The New York Times.* To learn more about *The New York Times,* visit them on the Web at **http://www.nytimes.com**.

Using the search-by-subject archive is easy. Simply type a word, or multiple words separated by commas, into the search box and click "go." You will see a list of articles that have appeared in the *New York Times* over the last year, sorted by most recent article first. You can further refine your search as needed. Articles can be printed or saved for later use in your research assignment. Be sure to review the citation rules for how to cite a newspaper article in endnotes or a bibliography.

"Best of the Web" Link Library

The third database included on Research Navigator™, Link Library, is a collection of Web links, organized by academic subject and key terms. To use this database, simply select an academic subject from the dropdown list, and then find the key term for the topic you are searching. Click on the key term and see a list of five to seven editorially reviewed Web sites that offer educationally relevant and reliable content. For example, if your research topic is "Allergies," you may want to select the academic subject Biology and then click on "Allergies" for links to web sites that explore this topic. Simply click on the alphabet bar to view other key terms in Biology, and their corresponding links. The web links in Link Library are monitored and updated each week, reducing your incidence of finding "dead" links.

Research Navigator Guide: Sociology

Using Your Library

After you have selected your topic and gathered source material from the three databases of content on Research Navigator™, you may need to complete your research by going to your school library. Research Navigator™ does not try to replace the library, but rather helps you understand how to use library resources effectively and efficiently.

You may put off going to the library to complete research assignments or research papers because the library can seem overwhelming. Research Navigator™ provides a bridge to the library by taking you through a simple step-by-step overview of how to make the most of your library time. Written by a library scientist, the *Using Your Library* tab explains:

- Major types of libraries
- What the library has to offer
- How to choose the right library tools for a project
- The research process
- How to make the most of research time in the library

In addition, when you are ready to use the library to complete a research assignment or research paper, Research Navigator™ includes 31 discipline-specific "library guides" for you to use as a roadmap. Each guide includes an overview of the discipline's major subject databases, online journals, and key associations and newsgroups.

For more information and detailed walk-throughs, please visit
www.ablongman.com/aboutRN

Research Navigator Guide: Sociology

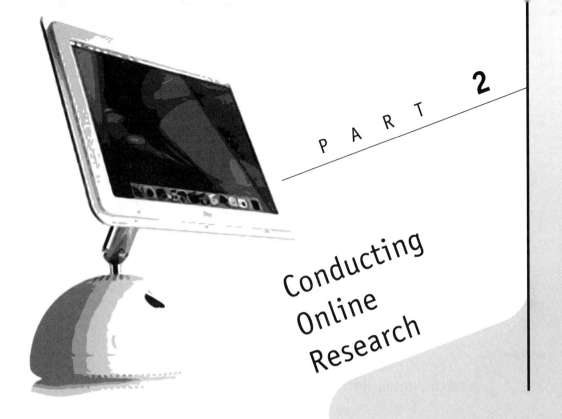

Conducting
Online
Research

Finding Sources:
Search Engines and Subject Directories

Your professor has just given you an assignment to give a five minute
speech on the topic "gun control." After a (hopefully brief) panic attack,
you begin to think of what type of information you need before you can
write the speech. To provide an interesting introduction, you decide to in-
volve your class by taking a straw poll of their views for and against gun
control, and to follow this up by giving some statistics on how many Americans favor (and oppose) gun control legislation and then by outlining the
arguments on both sides of the issue. If you already know the correct URL
for an authoritative Web site like Gallup Opinion Polls (www.gallup.com)
or other sites you are in great shape! However, what do you do when you
don't have a clue as to which Web site would have information on your
topic? In these cases, many, many people routinely (and mistakenly) go to
Yahoo! and type in a single term (e.g., guns). This approach is sure to bring
first a smile to your face when the results offer you 200,874 hits on your
topic, but just as quickly make you grind your teeth in frustration when you
start scrolling down the hit list and find sites that range from gun dealer-
ships, to reviews of the video "Young Guns," to aging fan sites for "Guns
and Roses."

Finding information on a specific topic on the Web is a challenge. The more intricate your research need, the more difficult it is to find the one or two Web sites among the billions that feature the information you want. This section is designed to help you to avoid frustration and to focus in on the right site for your research by using search engines, subject directories, and meta-sites.

Search Engines

Search engines (sometimes called search services) are becoming more numerous on the Web. Originally, they were designed to help users search the Web by topic. More recently, search engines have added features which enhance their usefulness, such as searching a particular part of the Web (e.g., only sites of educational institutions—dot.edu), retrieving just one site which the search engine touts as most relevant (like Ask Jeeves {www.aj.com}), or retrieving up to 10 sites which the search engine rank as most relevant (like Google {www.google.com}).

Search Engine Defined

According to Cohen (1999):

"A search engine service provides a searchable database of Internet files collected by a computer program called a wanderer, crawler, robot, worm, or spider. Indexing is created from the collected files, and the results are presented in a schematic order. There are no selection criteria for the collection of files.

A search service therefore consists of three components: (1) a spider, a program that traverses the Web from link to link, identifying and reading pages; (2) an index, a database containing a copy of each Web page gathered by the spider; and (3) a search engine mechanism, software that enables users to query the index and then returns results in a schematic order (p. 31)."

One problem students often have in their use of search engines is that they are deceptively easy to use. Like our example "guns," no matter what is typed into the handy box at the top, links to numerous Web sites appear instantaneously, lulling students into a false sense of security. Since so much was retrieved, surely SOME of it must be useful. WRONG! Many Web sites retrieved will be very light on substantive content, which is not what you need for most academic endeavors. Finding just the right Web site has been likened to finding diamonds in the desert.

As you can see by the definition above, one reason for this is that most search engines use indexes developed by machines. Therefore they are indexing terms not concepts. The search engine cannot tell the difference between the keyword "crack" to mean a split in the sidewalk and "crack" referring to crack cocaine. To use search engines properly takes some skill, and this chapter will provide tips to help you use search engines more effectively. First, however, let's look at the different types of search engines with examples:

TYPES OF SEARCH ENGINES

TYPE	DESCRIPTION	EXAMPLES
1st Generation	• Non-evaluative, do not evaluate results in terms of content or authority. • Return results ranked by relevancy alone (number of times the term(s) entered appear, usually on the first paragraph or page of the site)	AltaVista (www.altavista.com/) Excite (www.excite.com) HotBot (www.HotBot.com) Infoseek (guide.infoseek.com) Ixquick Metasearch (ixquick.com) Lycos (www.lycos.com)
2nd Generation	• More creative in displaying results. • Results are ordered by characteristics such as: concept, document type, Web site, popularity, etc. rather than relevancy.	Ask Jeeves (www.aj.com/) Direct Hit (www.directhit.com/) Google! (www.google.com/) HotLinks (www.hotlinks.com/) Simplifind (www.simpli.com/) SurfWax (www.surfwax.com/) Also see Meta-Search engines below. EVALUATIVE SEARCH ENGINES About.Com (www.about.com) WebCrawler (www.webcrawler.com)
Commercial Portals	• Provide additional features such as: customized news, stock quotations, weather reports, shopping, etc. • They want to be used as a "one stop" Web guide. • They profit from prominent advertisements and fees charged to featured sites.	GONetwork (www.go.com/) Google Web Directory (directory.google.com/) LookSmart (www.looksmart.com/) My Starting Point (www.stpt.com/) Open Directory Project (dmoz.org/) NetNow (www.inetnow.com) Yahoo! (www.yahoo.com/)
Meta-Search Engines	Run searches on multiple search engines.	There are different types of meta-search engines. See the next 2 boxes.

(continued)

Research Navigator Guide: Sociology

TYPES OF SEARCH ENGINES, *continued*		
TYPE	**DESCRIPTION**	**EXAMPLES**
Meta-Search Engines *Integrated Result*	• Display results for search engines in one list. • Duplicates are removed. • Only portions of results from each engine are returned.	Beaucoup.com (www.beaucoup.com/) Highway 61 (www.highway61.com) Cyber411(www.cyber411. com/) Mamma (www.mamma.com/) MetaCrawler (www. metacrawler.com/) Visisimo (www.vivisimo.com) Northern Light (www.nlsearch.com/) SurfWax (www.surfwax.com)
Meta-Search Engines *Non-Integrated Results*	• Comprehensive search. • Displays results from each search engine in separate results sets. • Duplicates remain. • You must sift through all the sites.	Dogpile (www.dogpile.com) Global Federated Search (jin.dis.vt.edu/fedsearch/) GoHip (www.gohip.com) Searchalot (www.searchalot.com) 1Blink (www.1blink.com) ProFusion (www. profusion.com/)

QUICK TIPS FOR MORE EFFECTIVE USE OF SEARCH ENGINES

1. Use a search engine:
   - When you have a narrow idea to search.
   - When you want to search the full text of countless Web pages
   - When you want to retrieve a large number of sites
   - When the features of the search engine (like searching particular parts of the Web) help with your search

2. Always use Boolean Operators to combine terms. Searching on a single term is a sure way to retrieve a very large number of Web pages, few, if any, of which are on target.
   - Always check search engine's HELP feature to see what symbols are used for the operators as these vary (e.g., some engines use the & or + symbol for AND).
   - Boolean Operators include:
     AND to narrow search and to make sure that **both** terms are included
       e.g:, children AND violence
     OR to broaden search and to make sure that **either** term is included
       e.g., child OR children OR juveniles
     NOT to **exclude** one term
       e.g., eclipse NOT lunar

Research Navigator Guide: Sociology

3. Use appropriate symbols to indicate important terms and to indicate phrases (Best Bet for Constructing a Search According to Cohen (1999): Use a plus sign (+) in front of terms you want to retrieve: +solar +eclipse. Place a phrase in double quotation marks: "solar eclipse" Put together: "+solar eclipse" "+South America").

4. Use word stemming (a.k.a. truncation) to find all variations of a word (check search engine HELP for symbols).
   - If you want to retrieve child, child's, or children use child* (some engines use other symbols such as !, #, or $)
   - Some engines automatically search singular and plural terms, check HELP to see if yours does.

5. Since search engines only search a portion of the Web, use several search engines or a meta-search engine to extend your reach.

6. Remember search engines are generally mindless drones that do not evaluate. Do not rely on them to find the best Web sites on your topic, use *subject directories* or meta-sites to enhance value (see below).

Finding Those Diamonds in the Desert: Using Subject Directories and Meta-sites

Although some search engines, like WebCrawler (www.webcrawler.com) do evaluate the Web sites they index, most search engines do not make any judgment on the worth of the content. They just return a long—sometimes very long—list of sites that contained your keyword. However, *subject directories* exist that are developed by human indexers, usually librarians or subject experts, and are defined by Cohen (1999) as follows:

> "A subject directory is a service that offers a collection of links to Internet resources submitted by site creators or evaluators and organized into subject categories. Directory services use selection criteria for choosing links to include, though the selectivity varies among services (p. 27)."

World Wide Web Subject directories are useful when you want to see sites on your topic that have been reviewed, evaluated, and selected for their authority, accuracy, and value. They can be real time savers for students, since subject directories weed out the commercial, lightweight, or biased Web sites.

Metasites are similar to subject directories, but are more specific in nature, usually dealing with one scholarly field or discipline. Some examples of subject directories and meta-sites are found in the table on the next page.

Choose subject directories to ensure that you are searching the highest quality Web pages. As an added bonus, subject directories periodically check Web links to make sure that there are fewer dead ends and out-dated links.

Research Navigator Guide: Sociology

SMART SEARCHING—SUBJECT DIRECTORIES AND META-SITES	
TYPES—SUBJECT DIRECTORIES	**EXAMPLES**
General, covers many topics	Access to Internet and Subject Resources (www2.lib.udel.edu/subj/)
	Best Information on the Net (BIOTN) (http://library.sau.edu/bestinfo/)
	Federal Web Locator (www.infoctr.edu/fwl/)
	Galaxy (galaxy.einet.net)
	INFOMINE: Scholarly Internet Resource Collections (infomine.ucr.edu/)
	InfoSurf: Resources by Subject (www.library.ucsb.edu/subj/)
	Librarian's Index to the Internet (www.lii.org/)
	Martindale's "The Reference Desk" (www-sci.lib.uci.edu/ HSG/ref.html)
	PINAKES: A Subject Launchpad (www.hw.ac.uk/libWWW/irn/pinakes/pinakes.html)
	Refdesk.com (www.refdesk.com)
	Search Engines and Subject Directories (College of New Jersey) (www.tcnj.edu/~library/research/internet_ search.html)
	Scout Report Archives (www.scout.cs.wisc.edu/archives)
	Selected Reference Sites (www.mnsfld.edu/depts/lib/ mu~ref.html)
	WWW Virtual Library (http://vlib.org)
Subject Oriented	
• Communication Studies	The Media and Communication Studies Site (www.aber.ac.uk/media)
	University of Iowa Department of Communication Studies (www.uiowa.edu/~commstud/resources)
• Cultural Studies	Sara Zupko's Cultural Studies Center (www.popcultures.com)
• Education	Educational Virtual Library (www.csu.edu.au/education/ library.html)
	ERIC [Education ResourcesInformation Center] (ericir.sunsite.syr.edu/)
	Kathy Schrock's Guide for Educators (kathyschrock.net/abceval/index.htm)
• Journalism	Journalism Resources (bailiwick.lib.uiowa.edu/journalism/)
	Journalism and Media Criticism page (www.chss.montclair.edu/english/furr/media.html)
• Literature	Norton Web Source to American Literature (www.wwnorton.com/naal)
	Project Gutenberg [Over 3,000 full text titles] (www.gutenberg.net)

SMART SEARCHING, *continued*	
TYPES—SUBJECT DIRECTORIES	EXAMPLES
• Medicine & Health	PubMed [National Library of Medicine's index to Medical journals, 1966 to present] (www.ncbi.nlm.nih.gov/PubMed/) RxList: The Internet Drug Index (rxlist.com) Go Ask Alice (www.goaskalice.columbia.edu) [Health and sexuality]
• Technology	CNET.com (www.cnet.com)

Another closely related group of sites are the *Virtual Library sites,* also referred to as Digital Library sites. Hopefully, your campus library has an outstanding Web site for both on-campus and off-campus access to resources. If not, there are several virtual library sites that you can use, although you should realize that some of the resources would be subscription based, and not accessible unless you are a student of that particular university or college. These are useful because, like the subject directories and meta-sites, experts have organized Web sites by topic and selected only those of highest quality.

You now know how to search for information and use search engines more effectively. In the next section, you will learn more tips for evaluating the information that you found.

VIRTUAL LIBRARY SITES	
PUBLIC LIBRARIES	
• Internet Public Library	www.ipl.org
• Library of Congress	lcweb.loc.gov/homepage/lchp.html
• New York Public Library	www.nypl.org
University/College Libraries	
• Bucknell	jade.bucknell.edu/
• Case Western	www.cwru.edu/uclibraries.html
• Dartmouth	www.dartmouth.edu/~library
• Duke	www.lib.duke.edu/
• Franklin & Marshall	www.library.fandm.edu
• Harvard	www.harvard.edu/museums/
• Penn State	www.libraries.psu.edu
• Princeton	infoshare1.princeton.edu
• Stanford	www.slac.stanford.edu/FIND/spires.html
• ULCA	www.library.ucla.edu

(continued)

Research Navigator Guide: Sociology

VIRTUAL LIBRARY SITES, *continued*

PUBLIC LIBRARIES

Other
• Perseus Project [subject specific—classics, supported by grants from corporations and educational institutions] www.perseus.tufts.edu

BIBLIOGRAPHY FOR FURTHER READING

Books

Basch, Reva. (1996). Secrets of the Super Net Searchers.

Berkman, Robert I. (2000). *Find It Fast: How to Uncover Expert Information on Any Subject Online or in Print.* NY: HarperResource.

Glossbrenner, Alfred & Glossbrenner, Emily. (1999). *Search Engines for the World Wide Web,* 2nd Ed. Berkeley, CA: Peachpit Press.

Hock, Randolph, & Berinstein, Paula.. (1999). *The Extreme Searcher's Guide to Web Search Engines: A Handbook for the Serious Searcher.* Information Today, Inc.

Miller, Michael. *Complete Idiot's Guide to Yahoo!* (2000). Indianapolis, IN: Que.

Miller, Michael. *Complete Idiot's Guide to Online Search Secrets.* (2000). Indianapolis, IN: Que.

Paul, Nora, Williams, Margot, & Hane, Paula. (1999). *Great Scouts!: CyberGuides for Subject Searching on the Web.* Information Today, Inc.

Radford, Marie, Barnes, Susan, & Barr, Linda (2001). *Web Research: Selecting, Evaluating, and Citing* Boston. Allyn and Bacon.

Journal Articles

Cohen, Laura B. (1999, August). The Web as a research tool: Teaching strategies for instructors. *CHOICE Supplement* 3, 20–44.

Cohen, Laura B. (August 2000). Searching the Web: The Human Element Emerges. *CHOICE Supplement 37,* 17–31.

Introna, Lucas D., & Nissenbaum, Helen. (2000). Shaping the web: Why the politics of search engines matters. The Information Society, Vol. 16, No. 3, pp. 169–185.

Evaluating Sources on the Web

Congratulations! You've found a great Web site. Now what? The Web site you found seems like the perfect Web site for your research. But, are you sure? Why is it perfect? What criteria are you using to determine whether this Web site suits your purpose?

Think about it. Where else on earth can anyone "publish" information regardless of the *accuracy, currency,* or *reliability* of the information? The

Research Navigator Guide: Sociology

Internet has opened up a world of opportunity for posting and distributing information and ideas to virtually everyone, even those who might post misinformation for fun, or those with ulterior motives for promoting their point of view. Armed with the information provided in this guide, you can dig through the vast amount of useless information and misinformation on the World Wide Web to uncover the valuable information. Because practically anyone can post and distribute their ideas on the Web, you need to develop a new set of *critical thinking skills* that focus on the evaluation of the quality of information, rather than be influenced and manipulated by slick graphics and flashy moving java script.

Before the existence of online sources, the validity and accuracy of a source was more easily determined. For example, in order for a book to get to the publishing stage, it must go through many critiques, validation of facts, reviews, editorial changes and the like. Ownership of the information in the book is clear because the author's name is attached to it. The publisher's reputation is on the line too. If the book turns out to have incorrect information, reputations and money can be lost. In addition, books available in a university library are further reviewed by professional librarians and selected for library purchase because of their accuracy and value to students. Journal articles downloaded or printed from online subscription services, such as Infotrac, ProQuest, EbscoHost, or other fulltext databases, are put through the same scrutiny as the paper versions of the journals.

On the World Wide Web, however, Internet service providers (ISPs) simply give Web site authors a place to store information. The Web site author can post information that may not be validated or tested for accuracy. One mistake students typically make is to assume that all information on the Web is of equal value. Also, in the rush to get assignments in on time, students may not take the extra time to make sure that the information they are citing is accurate. It is easy just to cut and paste without really thinking about the content in a critical way. However, to make sure you are gathering accurate information and to get the best grade on your assignments, it is vital that you develop your critical ability to sift through the dirt to find the diamonds.

Web Evaluation Criteria

So, here you are, at this potentially great site. Let's go though some ways you can determine if this site is one you can cite with confidence in your research. Keep in mind, ease of use of a Web site is an issue, but more important is learning how to determine the validity of data, facts, and statements for your use. The five traditional ways to verify a paper source can also be applied to your Web source: *accuracy, authority, objectivity, coverage,* and *currency.*

Evaluating Web Sites Using
Five Criteria to Judge Web Site Content

Accuracy—How reliable is the information?

Authority—Who is the author and what are his or her credentials?

Objectivity—Does the Web site present a balanced or biased point of view?

Coverage—Is the information comprehensive enough for your needs?

Currency—Is the Web site up to date?

Use additional criteria to judge Web site content, including

- **Publisher, documentation, relevance, scope, audience, appropriateness of format**, and **navigation**
- Judging whether the site is made up of **primary (original) or secondary (interpretive) sources**
- Determining whether the information is **relevant** to your research

Content Evaluation

Accuracy. Internet searches are not the same as searches of library databases because much of the information on the Web has not been edited, whereas information in databases has. It is your responsibility to make sure that the information you use in a school project is accurate. When you examine the content on a Web site or Web page, you can ask yourself a number of questions to determine whether the information is accurate.

1. Is the information reliable?
2. Do the facts from your other research contradict the facts you find on this Web page?
3. Do any misspellings and/or grammar mistakes indicate a hastily put together Web site that has not been checked for accuracy?
4. Is the content on the page verifiable through some other source? Can you find similar facts elsewhere (journals, books, or other online sources) to support the facts you see on this Web page?
5. Do you find links to other Web sites on a similar topic? If so, check those links to ascertain whether they back up the information you see on the Web page you are interested in using.
6. Is a bibliography of additional sources for research provided? Lack of a bibliography doesn't mean the page isn't accurate, but having one allows you further investigation points to check the information.
7. Does the site of a research document or study explain how the data was collected and the type of research method used to interpret the data?

If you've found a site with information that seems too good to be true, it may be. You need to verify information that you read on the Web by cross-checking against other sources.

Authority. An important question to ask when you are evaluating a Web site is, "Who is the author of the information?" Do you know whether the author is a recognized authority in his or her field? Biographical information, references to publications, degrees, qualifications, and organizational affiliations can help to indicate an author's authority. For example, if you are researching the topic of laser surgery citing a medical doctor would be better than citing a college student who has had laser surgery.

The organization sponsoring the site can also provide clues about whether the information is fact or opinion. Examine how the information was gathered and the research method used to prepare the study or report. Other questions to ask include:

1. Who is responsible for the content of the page? Although a webmaster's name is often listed, this person is not necessarily responsible for the content.
2. Is the author recognized in the subject area? Does this person cite any other publications he or she has authored?
3. Does the author list his or her background or credentials (e.g., Ph.D. degree, title such as professor, or other honorary or social distinction)?
4. Is there a way to contact the author? Does the author provide a phone number or email address?
5. If the page is mounted by an organization, is it a known, reputable one?
6. How long has the organization been in existence?
7. Does the URL for the Web page end in the extension .edu or .org? Such extensions indicate authority compared to dotcoms (.com), which are commercial enterprises. (For example, www.cancer.com takes you to an online drugstore that has a cancer information page; www.cancer.org is the American Cancer Society Web site.)

A good idea is to ask yourself whether the author or organization presenting the information on the Web is an authority on the subject. If the answer is no, this may not be a good source of information.

Objectivity. Every author has a point of view, and some views are more controversial than others. Journalists try to be objective by providing both sides of a story. Academics attempt to persuade readers by presenting a logical argument, which cites other scholars' work. You need to look for two sided arguments in news and information sites. For academic papers, you need to determine how the paper fits within its discipline and whether the author is using controversial methods for reporting a conclusion.

Authoritative authors situate their work within a larger discipline. This background helps readers evaluate the author's knowledge on a particular subject. You should ascertain whether the author's approach is controversial and whether he or she acknowledges this. More important, is the information being presented as fact or opinion? Authors who argue for their position provide readers with other sources that support their arguments. If no sources are cited, the material may be an opinion piece rather than an objective presentation of information. The following questions can help you determine objectivity:

1. Is the purpose of the site clearly stated, either by the author or the organization authoring the site?
2. Does the site give a balanced viewpoint or present only one side?
3. Is the information directed toward a specific group of viewers?
4. Does the site contain advertising?
5. Does the copyright belong to a person or an organization?
6. Do you see anything to indicate who is funding the site?

Everyone has a point of view. This is important to remember when you are using Web resources. A question to keep asking yourself is, What is the bias or point of *view* being expressed here?

Coverage.   Coverage deals with the breadth and depth of information presented on a Web site. Stated another way, it is about how much information is presented and how detailed the information is. Looking at the site map or index can give you an idea about how much information is contained on a site. This isn't necessarily bad. Coverage is a criteria that is tied closely to *your* research requirement. For one assignment, a given Web site may be too general for your needs. For another assignment, that same site might be perfect. Some sites contain very little actual information because pages are filled with links to other sites. Coverage also relates to objectivity You should ask the following questions about coverage:

1. Does the author present both sides of the story or is a piece of the story missing?
2. Is the information comprehensive enough for your needs?
3. Does the site cover too much, too generally?
4. Do you need more specific information than the site can provide?
5. Does the site have an objective approach?

In addition to examining what is covered on a Web site, equally revealing is what is not covered. Missing information can reveal a bias in the material. Keep in mind that you are evaluating the information on a Web site for your research requirements.

Currency.   Currency questions deal with the timeliness of information. However, currency is more important for some topics than for others. For example, currency is essential when you are looking for technology related topics and current events. In contrast, currency may not be relevant when you are doing research on Plato or Ancient Greece. In terms of Web sites, currency also pertains to whether the site is being kept up to date and links are being maintained. Sites on the Web are sometimes abandoned by their owners. When people move or change jobs, they may neglect to remove theft site from the company or university server. To test currency ask the following questions:

1. Does the site indicate when the content was created?
2. Does the site contain a last revised date? How old is the date? (In the early part of 2001, a university updated their Web site with a "last updated" date of 1901! This obviously was a Y2K problem, but it does point out the need to be observant of such things!)
3. Does the author state how often he or she revises the information? Some sites are on a monthly update cycle (e.g., a government statistics page).
4. Can you tell specifically what content was revised?
5. Is the information still useful for your topic? Even if the last update is old, the site might still be worthy of use *if* the content is still valid for your research.

Relevancy to Your Research: Primary versus Secondary Sources

Some research assignments require the use of primary (original) sources. Materials such as raw data, diaries, letters, manuscripts, and original accounts of events can be considered primary material. In most cases, these historical documents are no longer copyrighted. The Web is a great source for this type of resource.

Information that has been analyzed and previously interpreted is considered a secondary source. Sometimes secondary sources are more appropriate than primary sources. If, for example, you are asked to analyze a topic or to find an analysis of a topic, a secondary source of an analysis would be most appropriate. Ask yourself the following questions to determine whether the Web site is relevant to your research:

1. Is it a primary or secondary source?
2. Do you need a primary source?
3. Does the assignment require you to cite different types of sources? For example, are you supposed to use at least one book, one journal article, and one Web page?

You need to think critically, both visually and verbally, when evaluating Web sites. Because Web sites are designed as multimedia hypertexts, nonlinear texts, visual elements, and navigational tools are added to the evaluation process.

Help in Evaluating Web Sites. One shortcut to finding high-quality Web sites is using subject directories and meta-sites, which select the Web sites they index by similar evaluation criteria to those just described. If you want to learn more about evaluating Web sites, many colleges and universities provide sites that help you evaluate Web resources. The following list contains some excellent examples of these evaluation sites:

- Evaluating Quality on the Net—Hope Tillman, Babson College
  www.hopetillman.com/findqual.html
- Critical Web Evaluation—Kurt W. Wagner, William Paterson University of New Jersey
  euphrates.wpunj.edu/faculty/wagnerk/
- Evalation Criteria—Susan Beck, New Mexico State University
  lib.nmsu.edu/instruction/evalcrit.html
- A Student's Guide to Research with the WWW
  www.slu.edu/departments/english/research/
- Evaluating Web Pages: Questions to Ask & Strategies for Getting the Answers
  www.lib.berkeley.edu/TeachingLib/Guides/Internet/
  EvalQuestions.html

Critical Evaluation Web Sites

WEB SITE AND URL	SOURCE
Critical Thinking in an Online World **www.library.ucsb.edu/untangle/** **jones.html**	*Paper from "Untangling the Web" 1996*
Educom Review: Information **www.educause.edu/pub/er/review/** **reviewArticles/31231.html**	*EDUCAUSE Literacy as a Liberal Art (1996 article)*
Evaluating Information Found on the Internet **MiltonsWeb.mse.jhu.edu/** **research/education/net.html**	*University of Utah Library*
Evaluating Web Sites **www.lib.purdue.edu/InternetEval**	*Purdue University Library*
Evaluating Web Sites **www.lehigh.edu/~inref/guides/** **evaluating.web.html**	*Lehigh University*
ICONnect: Curriculum Connections Overview **www.ala.org/ICONN/evaluate.html**	*American Library Association's technology education initiative*
Kathy Schrock's ABC's of Web Site Evaluation **www.kathyschrock.net/abceval/**	*Author's Web site*

Kids Pick the best of the Web
"Top 10: Announced"
www.ala.org/news/topkidpicks.html

American Library Association initiative underwritten by Microsoft (1998)

Resource Selection and Information Evaluation
alexia.lis.uiuc.edu/~janicke/ InfoAge.html

Univ of Illinois, Champaign-Urbana (Librarian)

Testing the Surf: Criteria for Evaluating Internet Information Sources
info.lib.uh.edu/pr/v8/n3/ smit8n3.html

University of Houston Libraries

Evaluating Web Resources
www2.widener.edu/ Wolfgram-Memorial-Library/ webevaluation/webeval.htm

Widener University Library

UCLA College Library Instruction: Thinking Critically about World Wide Web Resources
www.library.ucla.edu/libraries/ college/help/critical/

UCLA Library

UG OOL: Judging Quality on the Internet
www.open.uoguelph.ca/resources/ skills/judging.html

University of Guelph

Web Evaluation Criteria
lib.nmsu.edu/instruction/ evalcrit.html

New Mexico State University Library

Web Page Credibility Checklist
www.park.pvt.k12.md.us/academics/ research/credcheck.htm

Park School of Baltimore

Evaluating Web Sites for Educational Uses: Bibliography and Checklist
www.unc.edu/cit/guides/irg-49.html

University of North Carolina

Evaluating Web Sites
www.lesley.edu/library/guides/ research/evaluating_web.html

Lesley University

Research Navigator Guide: Sociology

TIP: Can't seem to get a URL to work? If the URL doesn't begin with www, you may need to put the http:// in front of the URL. Usually, browsers can handle URLs that begin with www without the need to type in the "http://" but if you find you're having trouble, add the http://.

Documentation Guidelines for Online Sources

Your Citation for Exemplary Research

There's another detail left for us to handle—the formal citing of electronic sources in academic papers. The very factor that makes research on the Internet exciting is the same factor that makes referencing these sources challenging: their dynamic nature. A journal article exists, either in print or on microfilm, virtually forever. A document on the Internet can come, go, and change without warning. Because the purpose of citing sources is to allow another scholar to retrace your argument, a good citation allows a reader to obtain information from your primary sources, to the extent possible. This means you need to include not only information on when a source was posted on the Internet (if available) but also when you obtained the information.

The two arbiters of form for academic and scholarly writing are the Modern Language Association (MLA) and the American Psychological Association (APA); both organizations have established styles for citing electronic publications.

MLA Style

In the fifth edition of the *MLA Handbook for Writers of Research Papers,* the MLA recommends the following formats:

- **URLs:** URLs are enclosed in angle brackets (<>) and contain the access mode identifier, the formal name for such indicators as "http" or "ftp." If a URL must be split across two lines, break it only after a slash (/). Never introduce a hyphen at the end of the first line. The URL should include all the parts necessary to identify uniquely the file/document being cited.

  <http://www.csun.edu/~rtvfdept/home/index.html>

- **An online scholarly project or reference database:** A complete "online reference contains the title of the project or database (underlined); the name of the editor of the project or database (if given); electronic publication information, including version number (if relevant and if not part of the title), date of electronic publication or latest update, and name of any sponsoring institution or organization; date of access; and electronic address.

  The Perseus Project. Ed. Gregory R. Crane. Mar. 1997. Department of Classics, Tufts University. 15 June 1998 <http://www.perseus.tufts.edu/>.

If you cannot find some of the information, then include the information that is available. The MLA also recommends that you print or download electronic documents, freezing them in time for future reference.

- **A document within a scholarly project or reference database:** It is much more common to use only a portion of a scholarly project or database. To cite an essay, poem, or other short work, begin this citation with the name of the author and the title of the work (in quotation marks). Then, include all the information used when citing a complete online scholarly project or reference database, however, make sure you use the URL of the specific work and not the address of the general site.

Cuthberg, Lori. "Moonwalk: Earthlings' Finest Hour."
    <u>Discovery Channel Online</u>. 1999. Discovery
    Channel. 25 Nov. 1999 <http://www.discovery.com/
    indep/newsfeatures/moonwalk/challenge.html>.

- **A professional or personal site:** Include the name of the person creating the site (reversed), followed by a period, the title of the site (underlined), or, if there is no title, a description such as Home page (such a description is neither placed in quotes nor underlined). Then, specify the name of any school, organization, or other institution affiliated with the site and follow it with your date of access and the URL of the page.

Packer, Andy. Home page. 1Apr. 1998 <http://
    www.suu.edu/~students/Packer.htm>.

Some electronic references are truly unique to the online domain. These include email, newsgroup postings, MUDs (multiuser domains) or MOOs (multiuser domains, object-oriented), and IRCs (Internet Relay Chats).

Email. In citing email messages, begin with the writer's name (reversed) followed by a period, then the title of the message (if any) in quotations as it appears in the subject line. Next comes a description of the message, typically "Email to," and the recipient (e.g., "the author"), and finally the date of the message.

Davis, Jeffrey. "Web Writing Resources." Email to
    Nora Davis. 3 Jan. 2000.

Sommers, Laurice. "Re: College Admissions
    Practices." Email to the author. 12 Aug. 1998.

List Servers and Newsgroups.   In citing these references, begin with the author's name (reversed) followed by a period. Next include the title of the document (in quotes) from the subject line, followed by the words "Online posting" (not in quotes). Follow this with the date of posting. For list servers, include the date of access, the name of the list (if known), and the online address of the list's moderator or administrator. For newsgroups, follow "Online posting" with the date of posting, the date of access, and the name of the newsgroup, prefixed with "news:" and enclosed in angle brackets.

```
Applebaum, Dale. "Educational Variables." Online
    posting. 29 Jan. 1998. Higher Education
    Discussion Group. 30 Jan. 1993
    <jlucidoj@unc.edu>.
```

```
Gostl, Jack. "Re: Mr. Levitan." Online posting.
    13 June 1997. 20 June 1997
    <news:alt.edu.bronxscience>.
```

MUDs, MOOs, and IRCs.   Begin with the name of the speaker(s) followed by a period. Follow with the description and date of the event, the forum in which the communication took place, the date of access, and the online address. If you accessed the MOO or MUD through telnet, your citation might appear as follows:

```
Guest. Personal interview. 13 Aug. 1998.
    <telnet://du.edu:8888>.
```

For more information on MLA documentation style for online sources, check out their Web site at http://www.mla.org/style/sources.htm.

APA Style

The newly revised *Publication Manual of the American Psychological Association* (5th ed.) now includes guidelines for Internet resources. The manual recommends that, at a minimum, a reference of an Internet source should provide a document title or description, a date (either the date of publication or update or the date of retrieval), and an address (in Internet terms, a uniform resource locator, or URL). Whenever possible, identify the authors of a document as well. It's important to remember that, unlike the MLA, the APA does not include temporary or transient sources (e.g., letters, phone calls, etc.) in its "References" page, preferring to handle them in the text. The general suggested format is as follows:

Online periodical:

Author, A. A., Author, B. B., & Author, C. C.
(2000). Title of article. *Title of Periodical,*
xx, xxxxx. Retrieved month, day, year, from
source.

Online document:

Author, A. A. (2000). *Title of work.* Retrieved
month, day, year, from source.

Some more specific examples are as follows:

FTP (File Transfer Protocol) Sites.   To cite files available for downloading via FTP, give the author's name (if known), the publication date (if
available and if different from the date accessed), the full title of the paper
(capitalizing only the first word and proper nouns), the date of access, and
the address of the FTP site along with the full path necessary to access the
file.

Deutsch, P. (1991) Archie: An electronic directory
service for the Internet. Retrieved January 25,
2000 from File Transfer Protocol: ftp://
ftp.sura.net/pub/archie/docs/whatis.archie

WWW Sites (World Wide Web).   To cite files available for viewing or
downloading via the World Wide Web, give the author's name (if known),
the year of publication (if known and if different from the date accessed),
the full title of the article, and the title of the complete work (if applicable)
in italics. Include any additional information (such as versions, editions, or
revisions) in parentheses immediately following the title. Include the date
of retrieval and full URL (the http address).

Burka, L. P. (1993). A hypertext history of multiuser dungeons. *MUDdex.* Retrieved January 13, 1997
from the World Wide Web: http://www.utopia.com/
talent/lpb/muddex/essay/

Tilton, J. (1995). Composing good HTML (Vers. 2.0.6).
Retrieved December 1, 1996 from the World Wide Web:
http://www.cs.cmu.edu/~tilt/cgh/

Synchronous Communications (MOOs, MUDs, IRC, etc.).   Give the
name of the speaker(s), the complete date of the conversation being ref-
erenced in parentheses, and the title of the session (if applicable). Next,

list the title of the site in italics, the protocol and address (if applicable), and any directions necessary to access the work. Last, list the date of access, followed by the retrieval information. Personal interviews do not need to be listed in the References, but do need to be included in parenthetic references in the text (see the APA *Publication Manual*).

> Cross, J. (1996, February 27). Netoric's Tuesday
>   "cafe: Why use MUDs in the writing classroom?
>   *MediaMoo*. Retrieved March 1, 1996 from File
>   Transfer Protocol: ftp://daedalus.com/
>   pub/ACW/NETORIC/catalog

Gopher Sites. List the author's name (if applicable), the year of publication, the title of the file or paper, and the title of the complete work (if applicable). Include any print publication information (if available) followed by the protocol (i.e., gopher://). List the date that the file was accessed and the path necessary to access the file.

> Massachusetts Higher Education Coordinating Council.
>   (1994). Using coordination and collaboration to
>   address change. Retrieved July 16, 1999 from the
>   World Wide Web: gopher://gopher.mass.edu:170/
>   00gopher_root%3A%5B_hecc%5D_plan

Email, Listservs, and Newsgroups. Do not include personal email in the list of References. Although unretrievable communication such as email is not included in APA References, somewhat more public or accessible Internet postings from newsgroups or listservs may be included. See the APA *Publication Manual* for information on in-text citations.

> Heilke, J. (1996, May 3). Webfolios. Alliance for
>   Computers and Writing Discussion List. Retrieved
>   December 31, 1996 from the World Wide Web:
>   http://www.ttu.edu/lists/acw-1/9605/0040.html

Other authors and educators have proposed similar extensions to the APA style. You can find links to these pages at:

> www.psychwww.com/resource/apacrib.htm

Remember, "frequently-referenced" does not equate to "correct" "or even "desirable." Check with your professor to see if your course or school has a preference for an extended APA style.

Research Navigator Guide: Sociology

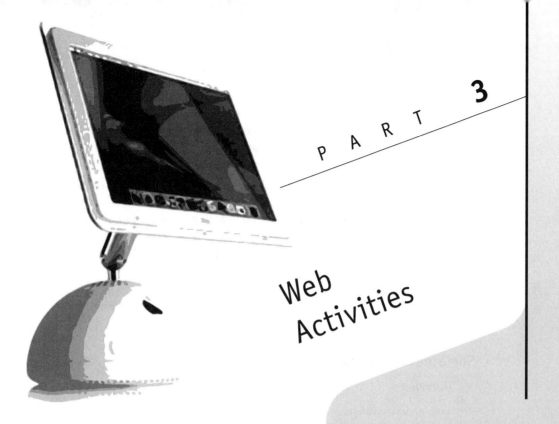

P A R T **3**

Web
Activities

Internet Activities for Sociology

Sociological Perspective 1

Overview

How do sociologists see the world? "What difference does it make to me?" you might ask. Let's examine the sociological perspective to see how it differs from other views of human social life.

Activity

Do you read a newspaper everyday? Your answer to this question is certainly a matter of personal choice. Whether you answer yes or no, a sociologist would no doubt be curious about your response. But, more likely a sociologist might ask a variety of questions. Are you like other Americans? What is happening to newspaper readership in our society? What forces produce this outcome?

Check the General Social Survey on **http://www.icpsr.umich.edu/ GSS/**

These data are presented in a table generated by a frequently used statistical package (SPSS). Look at the row (remember rows go across, columns go up and down) labeled EVERYDAY. For every year that data are presented, record the year and the percent of people who say they read a newspaper every day. Now answer the following:

1. For the most recent year, are most Americans like you in terms of daily readership?
2. Over the years for which data were collected, what is happening to the percentage of people who read a newspaper everyday? Now, use your sociological imagination—What are some of the social factors that have caused this?

If you're responding in general categories of factors (increased television viewing, more computers, etc.), you're probably thinking more sociologically.

Sociological Perspective 2

Overview

The sociological perspective is handy because it can be applied to so many different and interesting areas. Think about it for a minute. What areas could use a little sociology? Let's take a look at a list.

Activity

1. List some areas that interest you that you believe could be viewed sociologically.
2. Now, go to **http://www.pscw.uva.nl/sociosite/TOPICS/index. html**
3. Is there anything on your list that matches here? If so, click on it and review the findings.
4. If you can't make a connection, choose 3–5 of the ones at the site and follow the links. There's no telling where these links might lead!
5. What are the strengths and weaknesses of sociology's breadth?

Sociological Perspective 3

Overview

How do sociologists know anything? Sociologists are scientists who study human interaction at many levels. The methods and techniques employed usually fall into two categories: quantitative and qualitative. Let's compare these two research approaches

Activity

Let's start by looking at a common "quantitative" method used by sociologists: the survey. Go to **http://hammock.ifas.ufl.edu/txt/fairs/ 13467**

1. Read the discussion on selecting a data collection technique.
2. Now, move to the middle of the page and click on "comparison of three techniques."
3. What are the three survey techniques described here? How are they similar and different? Under what circumstances is it best to use each?

Now, let's turn to a common qualitative technique: focus groups. Go to **http://palette.ecn.purdue.edu/~ie486/Class/Lecture/lect13/ index.htm**

4. What is a focus group?

Then, go to **http://mime1.marc.gatech.edu/mm_tools/evaluation. html.** Scroll down to "Focus Group." Read the overview and go to the protocol. Using information from both links, answer the following:

5. How do focus groups compare with surveys? How are they similar and how are they different?
6. How could the two techniques complement each other?

Sociological Perspective 4

Overview

Sociology and sociologists maintain a vast network of resources, organizations, and individuals that support the field. Let's explore some of the organizations that support sociology.

Activity

To get an initial view of the breadth of sociological organizations and resources, go to **http://www.sociolog.com/**

1. Spend some time just investigating the information on this site.
2. Now, summarize the basic categories of information that you've found here.
3. Finally, make some comparisons:
   a. Compare two or more 6professional associations.
   b. Compare two or more regional associations, and
   c. Compare two or more organizations in different international locations.
4. Summarize your thoughts on the nature of the variety of these organizations.

Sociological Perspective 5

Overview

By now you are probably aware of sociology's breadth. The field easily extends from the interaction among "selves" to the interaction among societies. Let's get an understanding of the variety of topics that a professional sociologist might investigate.

Activity

One place to start is to identify the largest single professional organization for sociologists, the American Sociological Association. Go to **http://www.asanet.org/**

1. Once you have arrived, click on the list of sections in the ASA. Go to **http://www.asanet.org/Sections/general.html**
2. What are sections? What value do they have?
3. How many sections did you find? Pick 3–5 sections that might appear to be interesting to you. Why would these be of interest?
4. Use your sociological imagination—What do you think sociologists in each section investigate? Some of the sections are linked to the web site. Explore the ones that interest you.

OTHER SITES ON SOCIOLOGICAL PERSPECTIVE	
URL LINK	SUMMARY: WHO RUNS THE SITE? DESCRIPTION?

Applied Sociology 1

Overview

Practicing sociologists (and many other professionals as well) are called on to conduct program evaluations. After investing time, money and resources in a project, it would not be surprising or unreasonable to ask if the project "did what it was supposed to do." Evaluation skills are useful tools.

Activity

Go to the American Evaluation Association site at: **http://www.eval. org/** Evaluation design requires guidelines for implementation. Click on AEA Guiding Principles for Evaluators.

1. What are the major categories of guidelines that are recommended for project or program evaluation?
2. What are some of the sociological perspectives and methods that might be used in an evaluation?
3. What would be some of the obstacles for performing a good evaluation?

Applied Sociology 2

Overview

Whether you're presenting your sociological information to an academic audience or a business client, making a good presentation is essential. Having some basic presentation skills can be extremely valuable.

Activity

First, let's find something to present. Go to **http://nces.ed.gov/ pubsearch/pubsinfo.asp?pubid=2000022**

1. Review the material on this site. What are the key variables and information presented here?

Now, suppose you need to make a presentation of the findings on this site to a group of businessmen and businesswomen who have assembled because of their concern for providing realistic work opportunities for dropouts. How would you do it? Go to **http://angelfire.com/hi/rwm/ classes/general/presentation.html**

2. Review this site for pointers that would help you make your presentation.
3. Provide a brief outline of your presentation employing some of the suggestions on this site.

Applied Sociology 3

Overview

Practicing sociology means identifying, investigating and solving problems. There are many processes for problem analysis that can be valuable tools for you regardless of the career that you seek. Let's look at one of these.

Activity

Investigate the process for analyzing problems on **http://www.changedynamics.com/samples/probsolv.htm**

1. Review the process. What are its basic steps?
2. Compare this to the scientific method. How is it similar? How is it different?
3. Now, select a problem (whether from your workplace, college, family or your imagination). Use this process to analyze it.
4. What are the strengths and weaknesses of this process?

OTHER SITES ON APPLIED SOCIOLOGY	
URL LINK	SUMMARY: WHO RUNS THE SITE? DESCRIPTION?

How Sociologists Do Research 1

Overview

While sociologists and other social scientists often debate over the best tools to do research, none would doubt the wide variety of tools that are available. Let's turn to this large toolbox for a moment.

Activity

Go to **http://www.siu.edu/~hawkes/methods.html** Review the large spectrum of tools that are available to sociologists.

1. Sociologists need to learn a vast repertoire of tools and skills to do their work. What are some of the techniques and skills that look interesting to you?
2. Now, do a quick content analysis of the items that appear on this page. What categories of tools do sociologists need to learn?

How Sociologists Do Research 2

Overview

Sociologists are social scientists. If we emphasize the science part of social sciences, we realize that sociologists have a great deal in common with all scientists: biologists, psychologists, physicists, chemists, anthropologists, etc. The common thread is the use of the scientific method. Let's review this perspective.

Activity

Here are some Web sites that address the scientific method. What do they have in common?

Field research: **http://www.sru.edu/depts/artsci/ges/fstudies/ scmeth.htm**

Forms of the Scientific Method: **http://www.twingroves. district96.k12.il.us/ScienceInternet/ScientificMethod.html**

How Sociologists Do Research 3

Overview

Sociologists are known for doing survey research. While surveys aren't the only research method that we use, they are a valuable and common tool.

Activity

Survey research and its related skill, question writing, are difficult tasks. Part of the craft of becoming a sociologist is the ability to write good survey instruments. Before one can even write a good question, a researcher will need to reflect on a variety of factors influencing a survey. Go to **http://hammock.ifas.ufl.edu/txt/fairs/13467** Now answer the following questions:

1. What are reliability and validity? How do reliability and validity influence survey construction?
2. What is bias? How does bias impact on survey construction?
3. Now click on "Comparison of three techniques." Compare and contrast the three types of surveys identified here. State a research problem that could best be dealt with for each type of technique.

How Sociologists Do Research 4

Overview

Social scientists use a variety of tools to analyze data. Graphic and statistical tools are essential. This is a situation in which a few good tools can be extremely powerful.

Activity

In almost every data gathering experience you'll need to run some descriptive statistics. Go to **http://www.medschool.lsumc.edu/biom/ppt/ bascstat/tsld035.htm** and review the measures of central tendency. Since sociologists are interested in one number that stands for a group, these will be helpful.

Sometimes it's easier if we have a picture of information. Go to **http:// www.twingroves.district96.k12.il.us/ScienceInternet/ChartsGraphs. html** Scroll down to the middle of the page and review bar graphs, line graphs and circles (pie) graphs.

How Sociologists Do Research 5

Overview

Let's use this basic research tool, the survey, to deal with an application of the sociological perspective to a real life situation.

Activity

Go to **http://hammock.ifas.ufl.edu/txt/fairs/13471** and complete the following: You are an applied sociologist employed by a human resources department for a local hospital. The vice president of human resources has asked you to determine the level of worker satisfaction at all occupational levels in the hospital. You have two weeks to report your findings to the vice president. You decide to use a survey research technique. Apply the information in this link and decide which survey technique you would use and why you would use it.

OTHER SITES ON HOW SOCIOLOGISTS DO RESEARCH	
URL LINK	SUMMARY: WHO RUNS THE SITE? DESCRIPTION?

Research Navigator Guide: Sociology

Culture 1

Overview

Culture is a way of life and while each individual acts that way of life a little differently, we can improve our interaction with persons across cultures if we understand and respect the "ways" of life in which we find ourselves. This is one of the great strengths of sociology. Let's see how understanding culture can be of value to you.

Activity

You've decided to do some cross cultural consulting and determine that you would be better off if you met your clients in person rather than by Internet or telephone. Before you go on your trip, go to **http:// webofculture.com/**

1. Select three countries outside the United States that you plan to visit on your business trip.
2. For each country, review each of the following:
   a. Cuisine
   b. Currency
   c. Language
   d. Gestures
   e. Religion
   f. Select one or more items of your choice.
3. Compare and contrast the countries you have selected on the items listed above.
4. How would these differences influence your interaction with your client?

Culture 2

Overview

Comparing cultures is difficult. As you are learning, ways of life vary greatly. Traveling internationally will challenge your views of other cultures and your own. Let's make some comparisons.

Activity

Nations are not quite the same as cultures, but you can get a sense of cultural difference by comparing national similarities and differences. Go to **http://www.odci.gov/cia/publications/factbook/index.html**
Do the following:

1. What is the source of this web site? Any thoughts?

2. Now select two different continents in turn. Now select one country on each continent.
3. What categories of information are provided for each country?
4. Now compare and contrast the two countries across the categories of information provided?
5. How are they similar and different?
6. Now use your sociological imagination—What would it be like to live in each?

OTHER SITES ON CULTURE	
URL LINK	SUMMARY: WHO RUNS THE SITE? DESCRIPTION?

Socialization 1

Overview

Many factors influence the socialization of youth in a society. What are these factors? What impact do they have? Let's look at some indicators of youth in the United States.

Activity

Let's view a younger segment of the population. Go to **http://nces. ed.gov/pubs/yi/index.html**

1. Who runs this site? This site views 69 youth indicators. What are *indicators?* What are the categories of the indicators that you find here?
2. Now select at least one indicator from each category, click on it and review the data.
3. For each indicator that you have chosen, do the following:
   a. Write a brief 2–3 sentence paragraph that summarizes the condition presented by this indicator.
   b. Now use your sociological imagination: What impact will this have on the lives of the youth presented?

4. What are the strengths and weaknesses of assessing the condition of youth by using this indicator's strategy?

Socialization 2

Overview

Socialization is a process in which norms, values, and beliefs are passed to another person. In this process, this individual person becomes a social self. This process is life-long and we are often resocialized. Let's compare some processes and programs that intend to resocialize people.

Activity

Browse and compare the resocialization that is presented or discussed in each of the following three sites.

1. Compare and contrast the similarities and differences in the target (who?) of the resocialization, purpose, method, and anticipated outcomes for each.
http://www.tyc.state.tx.us/index.html (Click on "Basic Correctional Treatment–Resocialization")
http://www.parent-education.com/about.html
http://www.unicor.gov/placement/

How effective do you believe that each will be in resocializing? What social forces influence the success of this resocialization?

OTHER SITES ON SOCIALIZATION	
URL LINK	SUMMARY: WHO RUNS THE SITE? DESCRIPTION?

Social Structure 1

Overview

Social structure is a term sociologists use often. The term implies action driven by norms; persistent, patterned, organized action. These established and systematized patterns produce predictable outcomes. At a macro level, societies are viewed as structured on a number of factors—age, gender, race, and social class, to name a few. Let's look at an example.

Activity

While sociologists are quick to admit that an individual's action at the micro level relies on a measure of personal choice, we also hold that large portions of these choices are structured in and can be attributed to larger social structures. Go to **http://www.cdc.gov/nchs/**

1. Who runs this site?
2. Click on "FASTSTATS A TO Z" in the column on the left to see the wide range of topics covered by this agency.
3. Now go to **http://www.cdc.gov/nchs/fastats/pdf/hus99t61.pdf**
4. How do race, age and gender appear to impact the use of tobacco?
5. What changes in tobacco use do you see in the United States over the time frames presented?
6. What other variables might account for the patterned use of tobacco?

Social Structure 2

Overview

Using the concept of social structure can be empowering. In fact, implementing structure can be a valuable applied skill. While the structure is often viewed at a macro level, it has great importance at the "meso" or middle level as well. Let's look.

Activity

Let's first turn to an example of an effort to structure a work environment. Go to **http://www.emory.edu/ITD/Design/**

1. Who runs this site?
2. Browse through some of the links on the page.
3. Did sociologists design this structure?
4. Click on "social structure" and work through the links.
5. What elements are included in this structure, that is, what things were structured?
6. What can we learn from this example?

OTHER SITES ON SOCIAL STRUCTURE	
URL LINK	SUMMARY: WHO RUNS THE SITE? DESCRIPTION?

Social Interaction and Networks 1

Overview

Key to establishing relationships is social interaction. This interaction may occur in a variety of ways. Let's try our hand at one possible interaction.

Activity

http://cwolf.alaska.edu/~anlmg/soc/soc.htm attempts to connect sociology students by encouraging interaction.

1. What impact might this site have on students in sociology?
2. What value does it have to you?
3. How is this interaction different than a person-to-person discussion about sociology?

Social Interaction and Networks 2

Overview

The coming of cyberspace has changed interaction. Is face-to-face interaction gone forever? What differences can we expect from social interaction on the computer versus face-to-face? Let's see.

Activity

Here is one person's view of the differences in interaction—computer versus face-to-face. Go to **http://hsb.baylor.edu/ramsower/ais.ac.96/papers/rocco.htm**

1. What was investigated in this article?
2. What did the researcher discover?

3. Do you agree? What do you believe are the differences in these types of interactions?

Groups 1

Overview

Sociology is the study of interactions and, hence, groups. What does this mean? We call many clusters of people "groups." Let's get a definition.

Activity

Go to **http://campus.murraystate.edu/academic/faculty/frank. elwell/prob3/GLOSSARY/socgloss.htm** Elwell's Glossary provides some online definitions of key sociology terms. Now, find definitions for each of the following:

1. Social groups
2. Primary group
3. Primary group structure
4. Secondary group
5. Secondary group structure

Groups 2

Overview

Recently the importance of teamwork has made its way into American corporate life in the public and private sectors. Knowledge of groups that we get in sociology is a great link to understanding teams, and another reason to understand sociology. Let's look.

Activity

Go to **http://www.workteams.unt.edu/**

1. Who runs this site?
2. Browse the site. Follow some of the links.
3. What are some of the areas of interest explored here?
4. How can a general understanding of groups and interaction help you understand teams?
5. What occupations might use this skill?

OTHER SITES ON GROUPS	
URL LINK	SUMMARY: WHO RUNS THE SITE? DESCRIPTION?

Bureaucracy and Formal Organizations 1

Overview

Business Process Reengineering has become part of daily life within organizations. What is it? Would an understanding of sociology be useful in understanding and implementing it? Let's find out.

Activity

To get an understanding of business process reengineering go to **http://www.brint.com/BPR.htm**

1. Spend some time reviewing the links provided on this site.
2. Try to determine what BPR is. In your own words, what would you say BPR is?
3. Now link the sociology you have learned so far to the process of BPR. In what ways is an understanding of sociology helpful here?

Bureaucracy and Formal Organizations 2

Overview

Organizations take on many shapes and forms, or structures. Knowing the structure of an organization can be very helpful in understanding the nature of social interaction within it.

Activity

As a basic overview of organizational structure, go to **http://www.imaginiz.com/provocative/metaphors/models.html**

1. Identify and briefly describe the six models of organization presented here.

2. How would social interaction be different in each?
3. What are the strengths and weaknesses of each? Whose ideas are these anyway? Go to **http://www.yorku.ca/faculty/academic/gmorgan/index.html**

Bureaucracy and Formal Organizations 3

Overview

Who leads a formal organization? How can an organization be led? Leaders and leadership are topics of recent concern.

Activity

How can sociologists get involved in the process of developing leaders and leadership? Go to **http://www.exen.com/**

1. What is this organization? What is its purpose?
2. Consider the concepts that you've learned so far. What does sociology as a field and/or sociologists have to bring to an organization such as the one on this site?

OTHER SITES ON BUREAUCRACY AND FORMAL ORGANIZATIONS	
URL LINK	SUMMARY: WHO RUNS THE SITE? DESCRIPTION?

Deviance and Social Control 1

Overview

Crime is often viewed as one of the most obvious forms of social deviance. Law breaking has been the target of a great amount of social resources and public concern. What is the general nature of crime?

A very interesting starting point, and a useful site, is the Bureau of Justice Statistics. BJS is a warehouse of data on crime. Let's go to **http://www.ojp.usdoj.gov/bjs/**

1. Take some time just to explore the site. Now, return to the home page and click on "search this site."

When you get to the search engine, type in "trends."

    a. Select and review the trends in crime in the United States from 1965– the most recent date in the data that have some interest to you.

    b. How would you characterize the overall trend in crime?

    c. Are there any types of crime that have varied differently than the overall trend?

    d. Use your sociological imagination: What accounts for the differences in 3 and 4 above?

Deviance and Social Control 2

Overview

Deviance and society's response to it take numerous forms across cultures. Let's look at some variations on the theme of deviance: its definition and the response to it.

Activity

For each of these links, determine:

1. How is deviance determined?
2. Who decides what is deviant?
3. What response is expected?
4. How are these similar and different?

    Go to **http://www.umm.maine.edu/BEX/SocMod/SMMod3Deviance. html** Now, apply this conceptualization of deviance to a selection of items on this site: **http://web.mala.bc.ca/crim/dev/default.htm** (many possibilities here, choose among them).

5. Does the way one defines deviance have an impact on interpretation?

OTHER SITES ON DEVIANCE AND SOCIAL CONTROL	
URL LINK	SUMMARY: WHO RUNS THE SITE? DESCRIPTION?

Research Navigator Guide: Sociology

Stratification 1

Overview

Most of us are aware that income and wealth are not equally distributed in the United States. But, to what extent is this the case? If income inequality does exist, so what? Does it really change the way people behave, the way they live, their opportunities? Do subcultures of people, social class subcultures, or different ways of living emerge as a result of these differences?

Activity

What is the general distribution income in families in the United States? What percent of the total income does each 20 percent, that is each fifth, of the families in the United States get? To find out, go to **www.census. gov/hhes/income/incineq/p60tb1.html**

1. Describe the distribution of income in the United States
2. With respect to income distribution, are things getting more equal or less equal overall?
3. Use a sociological perspective. How did this distribution of income get this way? Why are the categories different? What caused the differences?
4. Use your sociological imagination—What impact does this income distribution have on society?

Stratification 2

Overview

We often look at social stratification—social layering—in our local community or in our nation. Does stratification exist globally? That is, does it exist across societies? How can we find out?

Activity

Start by going to the World Bank's indicators data base at **http://www. worldbank.org/data/countrydata/countrydata.html**

Now, to begin to determine if layering exists in the global village, create a table in which you compare the United Sates to three other countries (Note: this activity is not an attempt to reinforce stereotypes).

Put the following in your table:

1. One country that you believe has a standard of living similar to the United States.
2. One country that you believe has a standard of living lower than the United States, but not the lowest in the world.

3. One country that you believe has a standard of living among the lowest in the world.
4. Click on "compare only years with data," and compare these four countries (the United States and the three others) on the following indicators:
   a. Energy consumption per capita
   b. GNP per capita (US$)
   c. Illiteracy rate for the total population
   d. Life expectancy at birth for the total population
   e. Infant mortality rate
   f. Upper poverty line, headcount (percent of population)
5. Speculate from these indicators: How would life be different in each of these societies?
6. Is there reason to suggest that stratification exists globally?

OTHER SITES ON STRATIFICATION	
URL LINK	SUMMARY: WHO RUNS THE SITE? DESCRIPTION?

Social Class 1

Overview

A segment of the U.S. population lives in poverty. But, what does it mean to live in poverty?

Activity

The U.S. government has adopted a measurement scheme to identify those in poverty. Let's see how this is done. Go to **http://aspe.os.dhhs.gov/poverty/97poverty.htm**

1. What characteristics does the government use to determine a level of poverty?
2. What are the strengths and weaknesses of using this measurement device to determine poverty?

3. What characteristics would you use to make this distinction?

Social Class 2

Overview

Many Americans identify with the middle class. What does this mean? Let's take a look.

Activity

The Census Bureau addresses the notion of middle class in an interesting way. Go to **http://www.census.gov/hhes/income/midclass/midclsan. html**

1. How does the Census Bureau deal with the notion of middle class and income distribution?
2. There are other ways to define class. How would you apply them here?

OTHER SITES ON SOCIAL CLASS	
URL LINK	SUMMARY: WHO RUNS THE SITE? DESCRIPTION?

Race and Ethnicity 1

Overview

Publicly and in sociology we often discuss minority groups. What does it mean to have minority status? What impact does it have on people?

Activity

Go to **http://www.trinity.edu/~mkearl/race.html**

1. Who runs this site?
2. Read through the initial paragraphs. Keep reading until you read the discussion of minority groups.
3. What central features characterize a minority group?

4. Browse through this site and explore the links.
5. Do the racial and ethnic groups listed on this site conform to the minority group characteristics above? Which ones?
6. Must a minority group be a numerical minority? Explain your answer.

Race and Ethnicity 2

Overview

In a pluralistic culture, understanding the differences among the ways of life maintained by differing racial and ethnic groups is difficult, to say the least. Let's get some help in locating some references that compare selected racial and ethnic groups.

Activity

Go to the American Studies Web site on **http://www.georgetown. edu/crossroads/asw/**

1. Who runs this site?
2. Spend some time just investigating the range of offerings on this page.
3. Now, click on "Race and Ethnicity."
4. Review the content of this link. Which racial and ethnic groups are identified here?
5. For each group, investigate at least one link and indicate what you found.

OTHER SITES ON RACE AND ETHICITY	
URL LINK	SUMMARY: WHO RUNS THE SITE? DESCRIPTION?

Gender 1

Overview

The key to understanding gender differences between men and women from a sociological view is the patterned and different way that they are socialized. Are there really patterned differences?

Activity

To start, go to **http://www.academic.org/**

1. Who runs this site?
2. Browse through some of the links on the page.
3. According to those who run this site, what accounts for a large share of the differences between men and women?
4. This group recommends a change in the way we socialize girls. What are the strengths and weaknesses in things that they propose?
5. Would these proposed recommendations have an impact on boys, too? Explain.

Gender 2

Overview

Understanding changing gender roles is valuable information in understanding a changing society. Are there really issues that are gender specific? Let's consider this.

Activity

Start your search by going to **http://www.inform.umd.edu/EdRes/Topic/WomensStudies/**

1. Who runs this site?
2. Browse through some of the links on the page.
3. Now, scroll down to "gender issues" and click.
4. What issues are suggested to be largely "gender issues?" Why are they labeled this way?
5. What impact do these issues have on women? What impact do these issues have on men?

OTHER SITES ON GENDER	
URL LINK	SUMMARY: WHO RUNS THE SITE? DESCRIPTION?

Research Navigator Guide: Sociology

Age and Aging 1

Overview

We hear a great deal about the elderly population in the United States. What are the characteristics of this group? Let's find out.

Activity

Let's view the segment of the population that is over 65 years of age. Go to **http://www.census.gov/population/www/socdemo/age.html**

1. Describe the growth of this segment of the U.S. population. How will this group grow over the next 50 years?
2. What special needs will this group have as they age?
3. Will the society need to change to accommodate these needs?
4. What changes are likely?

Age and Aging 2

Overview

Taking a structural–functionalist approach, we would expect to see the emergence of an increasing number of voluntary and formal organizations in the presence of a major population change, such as the increasing number of elderly in American society. These organizations arise to meet the personal and social needs of this group. Has this happened for the elderly?

Activity

Check out the site at **http://www.aoa.dhhs.gov/aoa/resource.html**

1. Search or check the Table of Contents and review the resources listed on this site.
2. Categorize this list into 3–4 topics (such as Federal and state organizations, special needs organizations, and voluntary associations, for example).
3. Visit some of these sites in each of the categories that you've created above. For each site, indicate its purpose, the target population (the specific group it serves) and who funds it.
4. How would you characterize these resources?

Age and Aging 3

Overview

Many social forces will influence the nature of life for aging persons. What are some of these forces and how will they impact the lives of this group?

Activity

Review the site at **http://pr.aoa.dhhs.gov/aoa/stats/aging21**

1. Who wrote this article?
2. What are the four major categories of forces that will likely shape the lives of the elderly in the next century?
3. For each category, click on the link and review the social forces that are identified. Briefly note the impact that each is expected to have.
4. How would you summarize the life of the elderly in the next century?

OTHER SITES ON AGE AND AGING	
URL LINK	SUMMARY: WHO RUNS THE SITE? DESCRIPTION?

Health 1

Overview

Where could you go if you wanted to investigate health and wellness globally and within the United States? While you could search state-by-state, you might start at a central source. Let's look at some of these sources.

Activity

Let's start by looking globally. Go to **http://www.who.int/home-page/**

1. Who runs this site?
2. Click on search, and then search for a health related issue or illness.
3. What did you find? Are there any language barriers?

Now let's turn to the United States. Go to **http://www.cdc.gov**

1. Who runs this site?
2. Click on search, and then search for the same health related issue or illness that you investigated above.
3. What did you find?

4. Stop by the employment section and see if there are any interesting jobs.

Another source that might be interesting could be found at **http://www.cdc.gov/nchs/**

1. Who runs this site?
2. Click on NCHS Web Search, and then search for the same health related issue or illness that you investigated above.
3. What do you notice about this search site?

Health 2

Overview

How healthy is our society? How would we know? The need to understand the general health and wellness of a nation or a society is an important sociological focus. Let's take a look.

Activity

To start your briefing today, let's go to the White House. Go to **http://www.whitehouse.gov/fsbr/ssbr.html**

1. Now, click on "Health."
2. What are the indicators that are measured on this site?
3. Review each graph and accompanying data.
4. Summarize the information for each (What is happening?).
5. How would you characterize this method of measuring health in a society?

Health 3

Overview

Do you or your family have health insurance? If your answer is no, you know the concern you face when you need to have even basic health needs met. Healthy people have better chances of achieving their goals in life. But, is this access equal? Does everyone have the same chance to have some or all of their medical and health needs paid for by insurance? This Internet activity looks at stratification as a force in the access to health care.

Activity

Start your investigation by going to **http://www.census.gov/hhes/hlthins/cover95/c95taba.html**

1. What is the general distribution of health insurance in the United States? How many people have it, and what kind do they have? How many people have it and how many don't have it?
2. What are the major sources of health insurance?
3. Now go to **http://www.census.gov/hhes/hlthins/cover95/c95tabb. html**
4. What factors influence the access to health insurance?
5. What are the differences?
6. Use your sociological imagination—What impact would these differences (if they exist) have on society?

OTHER SITES ON HEALTH	
URL LINK	SUMMARY: WHO RUNS THE SITE? DESCRIPTION?

Education 1

Overview

Monitoring the educational well-being of a society is essential. Cross cultural and internal comparisons on just how well we're doing are often made by parents, teachers, politicians and individuals from all walks of life. Let's investigate some education indicators in the United States.

Activity

To start your briefing today, let's go to the White House. Go to **http://www.whitehouse.gov/fsbr/ssbr.html**

1. Now, click on "Education."
2. Name the indicators that are measured on this site?
3. Review each graph and accompanying data.
4. Summarize the information for each (What is happening?).
5. How would you characterize this method of measuring education in a society?

Education 2

Overview

The impact of the Internet on education will continue to challenge the way we learn. Let's look at some of the courses that are available in higher education.

Activity

Today you'll enter a different lecture hall. Go to **http://www. utexas.edu/world/lecture/** and/or **http://www.mcli.dist.maricopa. edu/tl/**

1. Use the search engine at this site to explore some of the courses that you are currently taking or might like to take. Type in the key word of the course you're interested in and see what happens.
2. Enter one of the courses that you have found. What is your assessment of the course at this site?
3. What impact will this type of learning have on education in the United States? What impact will it have globally? What impact will it have on you?

Education 3

Overview

Where can you get a good start when you're looking for data on education in the United States? Let's take a look at one clearinghouse for U.S. data on education.

Activity

On our review of education, start by going to **http://nces.ed.gov/**

1. Who runs this site?
2. Click on "Data and Surveys." Now review the list of research projects underway. Note that in most cases the results are not available. Rather, these are reviews of research and research design. How would you characterize the extent of the projects as presented here?
3. Now use the search engine on this site: **http://nces.ed.gov/search/ search.html**
4. Use the search engine at this site to explore some areas of interest. Start by typing "sociology."
5. Explore some of the data and data tables that are listed.
6. Identify and write a brief summary of the findings in a table of your choice.

Education 4

Overview

What is the nature of American education? Sometimes, amid the claims and controversy, it is difficult to know for sure. Let's take a look at U.S. education at three different levels.

Activity

1. Return to the National Center for Education and use their search engine at **http://nces.ed.gov/search/search.html**
2. Now type "elementary education." Search and browse through the information that emerges. Now, select one data source and summarize what you found.
3. Now type "secondary education." Search and browse through the information that emerges. Now, select one data source and summarize what you found.
4. Now type "postsecondary education." Search and browse through the information that emerges. Now, select one data source and summarize what you found.

OTHER SITES ON EDUCATION	
URL LINK	SUMMARY: WHO RUNS THE SITE? DESCRIPTION?

Family 1

Overview

Two-career families and the changing nature of the way we raise children in the United States have had many impacts. Did you ever wonder what do school-age children do with their time? Let's find out.

Activity

Explore the Fact Sheet on School-Age Children from the National Institute on Out-of-School Time at the Center for Research on Women, Wellesley College at **http://www.wellesley.edu/WCW/CRW/SAC/factsht.html**

1. How do school age children generally spend their time?
2. Why should anyone be concerned about this?
3. What problems or issues are associated with the use of time by school-age children?

Family 2

Overview

Single parent families are a part of family life in the United Sates. How prevalent is this form of family structure? What impact has it had on the way we raise children?

Activity

Interpret the information in the following table on this link: **http://nces.ed.gov/pubs/yi/y9611a.html**

This graph represents the data in the table above: **http://nces.ed.gov/pubs/yi/y9611c.html**

1. How does single parent familihood vary according to this graph?
2. How would you describe the prevalence of single parent families in the United States?
3. What impact, if any, has this had on early socialization?

OTHER SITES ON FAMILY	
URL LINK	SUMMARY: WHO RUNS THE SITE? DESCRIPTION?

Economy 1

Overview

Like many societal level or macro level characteristics, national economy is often measured using indicators. Indicators are measures that stand for something that is happening. Let's look at some indicators of the U.S. economy.

Activity

First list the indicators provided in the site **http://www.census.gov/briefrm/esbr/www/brief.html**

1. For each indicator, determine the direction the indicator is going. Is it basically going up, down or remaining the same over the time period provided?
2. Using the graphics, look for associations between the indicators. That is, as one indicator appears to be going up, what is happening to another indicator?
3. What useful information can sociology add to this type of analysis?

Economy 2

Overview

Consider the impact of labor unions on your standard of living. Labor unions have had a large impact not only on American economy, but also on our lifestyle. Let's see if we can get a sense of this impact.

Activity

Go to and review **http://www.labornet.org/**

1. List the topics that appear to be of interest to labor union members on this page.
2. Select 2–3 of these topics and follow their links. Briefly describe what you found in each.
3. Why do you believe that these topics were viewed as valuable?

Economy 3

Overview

Economic Institutions: What Does the Job Situation Look Like?
No doubt, one of the key reasons you're in college is to find a good job. Don't forget that jobs are roles—sets of expectations and obligations for human action. As such, they are connected to the economic institution which is affected by all other social institutions and societal forces. In or-

der to improve your chances in the job search, it would be wise to investigate the direction society and the economic institution is headed. Let's do this.

Activity

1. What will tomorrow's jobs look like? Let's find out by going to **http://stats.bls.gov/oco/oco2003.htm**
2. Who runs this site?
3. What is likely to occur with regard to employment growth between now and 2005?
4. What social forces are responsible for this change?
5. How might this change affect you?

Economy 4

Overview

Businesses and consumer groups actively use social science methods to track consumers. In many ways, this is a direct application of sociological perspectives and methods. Let's review an example of a business-oriented look at social patterns.

Activity

To start our search, go to **http://www.demographics.com/**

1. Now, click on one of the articles.
2. How was a sociological perspective used in this article?
3. Now, search some other articles. Scan 3–5 articles.
4. In general, how could sociology add value to the information presented?

OTHER SITES ON ECONOMY	
URL LINK	SUMMARY: WHO RUNS THE SITE? DESCRIPTION?

Religion 1

Overview

Sociology can be valuable in simply appreciating the breadth of religious beliefs in a society or cross-culturally. How many religious groups can you name? What do members of each group believe?

Activity

1. List the religious groups that you can think of right now. Take a few minutes with this.
2. Now go to **http://www.religionstolerance.org/var_rel.htm**
3. Browse through the site. Compare this list with yours. Any additions needed?
4. Now search the links for the religions that were originally in your list (the ones you knew about before this activity). Jot down anything new that you might discover.
5. Now pick 1–3 religions that you either had not heard of or whose beliefs you were uncertain about. What did you discover?
6. Use your sociological imagination: What impact does religion have on human social life?

Religion 2

Overview

Can a religious movement be a social movement? What is the breadth of religious movements? Let's find out.

Activity

1. Now go to **http://religiousmovements.lib.virginia.edu/profiles/**
2. Who runs this site?
3. These profiles seek to look at a variety of religious movements.
4. Scroll down the page and select 3–5 of these groups.
5. Compare and contrast them (their profile and beliefs).

How does this variety of religious belief impact society?

OTHER SITES ON RELIGION	
URL LINK	SUMMARY: WHO RUNS THE SITE? DESCRIPTION?

Politics 1

Overview

Political changes are fast breaking and are often difficult to monitor. They occur at each level of society: macro, middle range and micro. Let's see if we can grasp the range and the organization of political activity in the United States.

Activity

To start our tour of political structure, go to **http://www. politicalindex.com**

1. Who runs this site?
2. Now, investigate this site—click on areas of interest that span different levels of social organization: national/international, state and local.
3. Identify and briefly discuss what you found at each of these levels.
4. Pick some areas that look like they would be fun. What are they? What did you discover?
5. How does your understanding of sociology help you understand these political elements of our society?

Politics 2

Overview

Much of what we learn about politics is transmitted by the news media. Are the stories the same from newspaper to newspaper or television news station to news station? Let's see.

Activity

Many television network news services put their information on the Internet. Here are three different Internet sites:

Find a national or international level political story that appears on this service. Read the story and outline it. Pay attention to the way the story is presented. Now go to the remaining links. For each one:

http://www.abcnews.com/
http://www.msnbc.com/news/default.asp?cp1=1
http://www.cbsnews.com/now/section/0,1636,100-412,00.shtml

1. Determine if the story appears on the link.
2. If it does appear, compare and contrast it with the way the other stories were presented.
3. Do this for each of the remaining links.
4. Now, how were these news reports similar and different? If you found a difference, speculate as to why this might be so.

OTHER SITES ON POLITICS	
URL LINK	SUMMARY: WHO RUNS THE SITE? DESCRIPTION?

Population 1

Overview

Understanding human population—how many, what kind, and how fast it is growing—is an essential sociological tool. Let's get a general sense of some of the dimensions of human population.

Activity

Go to the Population Reference Bureau's site at **http://www.prb.org/**

1. Spend some time reviewing the links on the site.
2. Now try your hand at playing the Demographic Challenge Game by clicking the oval around the middle of the Bureau's home page. How did you do?

Population 2

Overview

Census data are valuable in understanding the past, present and future transitions in population. The U.S. Bureau of Census maintains a vast storehouse of data.

Activity

Go to **http://www.census.gov/**

1. For fun, click on the "Population Clock," the Current U.S. Population Count. How many people are in the U.S. population? (Indicate the time and date, too.)
2. Go back to the "Clock" 2 minutes later. What is the population now?
3. How did they do that?
4. Now click on "Search," and go to the Census search function.
5. Type in some key words or click on the first letter of a key word for which you would like some population information.
6. What did you find?

OTHER SITES ON POPULATION	
URL LINK	SUMMARY: WHO RUNS THE SITE? DESCRIPTION?

Urbanization and Community 1

Overview

Community can appear in a variety of environments. We often think about rural and urban communities within human societies, but let's turn to an emerging area in which community may reside.

Activity

As a contractor for NASA you have been asked (because of your sociological background, of course) to advise the agency director on the basic factors that NASA should address when considering the development of space communities. Go to **http://www.belmont.k12.ca.us/ralston/ programslitech/SpaceSettlement/index.html**

1. What factors would influence development of space communities?
2. How would space communities likely be different than Earth communities? How would they be similar?
3. Identify 3–5 critical areas to which the agency director should address her attention.

Urbanization and Community 2

Overview

Most of us would agree that life in cities is different than suburban or rural living. How is the size of a city associated with certain quality of life indicators? Let's find out.

Activity

1. How do the 25 cities with the largest population rank with regard to crime and infant mortality?
2. Access **http://www.census.gov/statab/ccdb/ccdb309.txt** with your browser.

Now, draw two graphs. On one, plot the rankings of city size on the x axis and the rank for the crimes/100,000 on the y axis. (When cities share the same rank, the next lower rank is omitted. CDP = census designated place.) Draw in a best-fitting straight line. On the second one, plot the rankings of city size on the x axis and infant death rates/1000 live births on the y axis. Draw in a best-fitting straight line for each graph.

1. Go to **http://www.census.gov/statab/ccdb/ccdb310.txt** and create two more graphs (repeat the procedure in #2 above) for the ranking of percent of elementary and high school enrollments and percent bachelor's degrees.
2. What did you discover? What associations did you find?
3. Use your sociological imagination—Why did this happen?
4. What other variables might influence the outcomes?

Urbanization and Community 3

Overview

While urbanization and its impact are important, we may neglect issues that face rural and agriculturally oriented communities. Take some time to investigate some of these issues in the United States and around the world.

Activity

Agricultural interests are often intertwined with rural interests. In our first step to investigate these interests, go to **http://www.card.iastate.edu**

1. Who runs this site? Why do you think this group maintains it?
2. Browse through the site.
3. Click on "emerging issues." Now, categorize the types of issues that you find here.
4. For this one point in time, what seem to be the issues of importance?
5. Click on some links that are most interesting to you? What are they? Why are they interesting?
6. How can sociology be used to understand these issues?

OTHER SITES ON URBANIZATION AND COMMUNITY	
URL LINK	SUMMARY: WHO RUNS THE SITE? DESCRIPTION?

Environment 1

Overview

Have you been hungry today? Food production is a good example of the interaction between human social systems and the environment. Let's look at attempts to monitor this interaction globally.

Activity

This site attempts to provide an early warning system on global food shortages. Go to **http://www.fao.org/WAICENT/faoinfo/economic/ giews/english/giewse.htm**

1. Who runs this site?
2. Browse through the site.
3. Review the Food Outlook for the most recent report. Click on "Highlights."
4. What is the status of food availability?
5. Use your sociological imagination: In this interaction between human societies and environment, what social forces and natural forces influence the availability of food?

Environment 2

Overview

Human societies interact with the environment in countless ways. What are some of the outcomes of this interaction? Let's look at a list of possibilities.

Activity

Go to **http://www.ulb.ac.be/ceese/meta/cds.html**

1. Who runs this site?
2. Browse through the list of issues and ideas on this site.
3. Select 2–3 of interest to you.
4. Now, for each item that you have selected consider the nature of the interaction of humans and the environment.
5. Take a systems (functionalist or ecological) point of view. Interpret your findings above. Now take a conflict view. How would you interpret these differently?

Environment 3

Overview

What action is taking place to deal with society's impact on environment? Let's take a walk around our environment and find out.

Activity

Go to **http://www.envirolink.org/EnviroLink_Library/**

1. Who runs this site?

2. Now take a walk around by clicking on water, air and the other icons presented.
3. Using your sociological perspective, how would you characterize the kinds of action listed here?
4. What forces in society are working for and against these activities?

OTHER SITES ON ENVIRONMENT	
URL LINK	SUMMARY: WHO RUNS THE SITE? DESCRIPTION?

Technology 1

Overview

What is "technology?" This term is often used. How does it relate to social change and changing human life? Let's investigate.

Activity

First define *technology*.

1. Either look for the term in a sociology textbook or go to **http://campus.murraystate.edu/academic/faculty/frank.elwell/prob3/GLOSSARY/socgloss.htm**
2. Now, go to **http://www.ctheory.com/**
3. What is presented on this site?
4. Browse through the site and choose 2–3 articles that might interest you.
5. In each article identify the technological factor(s) that is operating, and then describe that factor's impact on society as portrayed in the article.

Technology 2

Overview

The diffusion of new technology is often uneven. That is, it doesn't get to everybody at the same time. Some groups get it faster than others do.

There are many factors that influence this diffusion. Let's look at an attempt to address these factors.

Activity

Go to **http://streetlevel.iit.edu/**

1. Who runs this site?
2. Click on "general information." What is this site intended to do?

Just looking at the information on this site, what social factors that may influence the diffusion of technology are addressed on this site?

OTHER SITES ON TECHNOLOGY	
URL LINK	SUMMARY: WHO RUNS THE SITE? DESCRIPTION?

Collective Behavior 1

Overview

Public opinion is of concern to sociologists in general and those who study collective behavior specifically. An understanding of the collective perspective of a public can be a powerful tool.

Activity

Many organizations are involved locally, nationally and internationally in assessing public opinion. They view opinions at a variety of levels. Review public opinion at three different levels of social organization by going to these sites:

U.S. and International: **http://www.gallup.com/**
Primarily United States: **http://www.isr.umich.edu/src/projects.html** (Click on some of the SRC projects of interest to you)
http://www.icpsr.umich.edu/GSS/ (Click on "Trends in GSS Variables" and the "GSS Search Engine")
http://www.aacc.cc.md.us/csli (Click on "Surveys of . . . ")

1. Who runs these sites?
2. Review sample research (if available) on each site.
3. How can these data be used?
4. What are the strengths and weaknesses of collecting and using public opinion data?

Collective Behavior 2

Overview

What are social movements? We hear about them often. Let's take a look.

Activity

Go to **http://www.asanet.org/sections/collect.html** This is the section on Collective Behavior and Social Movements of the American Sociological Association.

1. Under the Welcome you'll find a description of just what is studied by persons who research social movements.
2. Given the information in #1, how would you define a social movement?
3. Now visit the following site: **http://www.wsu.edu:8080/~amerstu/ smc/smcframe.html**
4. Browse some of the links on social movements.
5. What are the similarities and differences among these groups?

OTHER SITES ON COLLECTIVE BEHAVIOR	
URL LINK	SUMMARY: WHO RUNS THE SITE? DESCRIPTION?

Social Movements 1

Overview

Social movements may exist at a variety of levels. Concern for changing some aspect of the social condition may exist next door, in your country, or around the world. Let's work through an example.

Activity

Go to **http://www.brown.edu/Departments/World_Hunger_Program/hungerweb/researchers.html**

1. Who runs this site?
2. Browse through the site. What problem is investigated here?
3. After reviewing some of the links at this site, go to **http://www.thp.org/thp/**
4. What does this group do?
5. At what levels (globally, nationally locally?) does it operate?
6. Now go to **http://www.action.org/**
7. What does this group do?
8. At what levels (globally, nationally locally?) does it operate?

Do these sites suggest the existence of a social movement? What is it? Use your sociological imagination: How effective is it? What social forces stand in its way?

OTHER SITES ON SOCIAL MOVEMENTS	
URL LINK	SUMMARY: WHO RUNS THE SITE? DESCRIPTION?

Social Change 1

Overview

Studying social change and its impact on humans and human societies is central to sociology. Change can come from many directions. Let's look at a change and speculate as to its likely impact.

Activity

Starting with the cloning of sheep, then cattle, then . . . ? Go to **http://www.sciam.com/explorations/030397clone/030397beards.html** Follow the arrows through the Web site.

1. What is your personal reaction to cloning?
2. What impact will cloning have on society?
3. What direct and indirect effects are likely to occur as a result of this scientific breakthrough?

Social Change 2

Overview

Increasingly, we have needed to reflect on the direct impact of societies beyond our own. This globalization of our view has been a source of social change.

Activity

Review this overview of a recent PBS special on globalization. Go to **http://www.pbs.org/globalization/home.html**

1. Review the summary of change and globalization. Do the makers of this site view globalization as having a positive or negative effect on other countries?
2. What changes have occurred in the U.S. and abroad as a result of globalization?
3. At what levels within the business world have these changes occurred?

OTHER SITES ON SOCIAL CHANGE	
URL LINK	SUMMARY: WHO RUNS THE SITE? DESCRIPTION?

The Future of Society 1

Overview

Analyzing trends, patterned and emerging changes, in society may give us some clues as to the society in which we are likely to find ourselves in the future. How could something that is likely to be happening in the future be realistically used in the present? Let's see.

Activity

Review this company report on the use of trend research to influence company focus. Go to **http://www.acm.org/sigs/sigchi/chi97/proceedings/briefing/rl.htm**

1. Read the report.
2. What trends did this company recognize that its leadership believed would have an impact on its product lines?
3. What was the actual process that the company used to brainstorm these trends and produce outcomes?
4. What did this company actually change or invent in response to the trends they identified?

The Future of Society 2

Overview

When people look into the near future, what do they see and how accurately do they see it? Let's look at one sociologist's attempt to characterize an emerging society.

Activity

Start this activity by going to **http://www.pscw.uva.nl/sociosite/TOPICS/Sociologists.html** At this site, click on "Bell, D."

1. Before you click on this article look at the Daniel Bell citation. When was this book (from which this section was derived) written?
2. Read the article.
3. How did Bell characterize the development of human societies over time; that is, what were the different societal types and how did life differ?
4. Has Bell's notion of the post-industrial society actually happened? Why do you think so?
5. What do you believe will happen after the post-industrial society?

The Future of Society 3

Overview

Many sociologists and futurists alike point to the "globalization of human action." The existence of a global social system is apparent. "How aware are you of daily events around the world? Let's take a quick global tour.

Activity

Go to this site **http://www.editorandpublisher.com/ editorandpublisher/business_resources/medialinks.jsp**

1. Who runs this site?
2. To make comparison easier, select "Newspaper."
3. Now pick one newspaper from each geographic area listed. For each:
   a. What is the name of the newspaper on this site?
   b. Browse the site.
   c. What were the top news stories today?

4. Now compare and contrast the stories. What are the similarities and differences across societies in today's news?
5. What impact does the ability to collect and compare these news stories have on your view of the world?
6. Suppose that you plan to travel to this site (in person). Would this information help you?

OTHER SITES ON THE FUTURE OF SOCIETY	
URL LINK	SUMMARY: WHO RUNS THE SITE? DESCRIPTION?

Research Navigator Guide: Sociology

Getting a Job with a Sociology Degree 1

Overview

Students graduating from college with a bachelor's degree in sociology may well ask: "What can I do with this degree anyway?" No doubt, you're asking this question regardless of your major in college. BA level sociology graduates have a great deal in common with other BA graduates. In many respects, job seeking and self-presentation skills are essential.

Activity

Sociologist Erving Goffman reminded us that we are constantly "presenting ourselves in everyday life." When looking for a job, this presentation can be critical. Go to **http://www.Careercity.com/**
On this site do the following:

1. How should someone dress for a job interview?
2. Construct a resume that integrates your current skills.
3. Write a short cover letter to your résumé.
4. Review the process for an electronic résumé.
5. What tips are provided for women looking for jobs?

Getting a Job with a Sociology Degree 2

Overview

Use your sociological skills to help you find a job, or at least shed some light on careers of interest to you. Let's examine some applications of sociological strategies to the job search process, and then some jobs that might be available.

Activity

1. First check out Catherine Mobley's "A Checklist for Job Hunting and Launching a Career in Applied Sociology" on **http://www.appliedsoc.org/m_jobs1.htm**
2. Work through some of her suggestions for strategies to get a job.

   Having completed this list, go to **http://www.politicalindex.com/sect23.htm**

1. Investigate the jobs in the various categories on this site.
2. Locate some jobs that might be interesting to you.
3. How would you apply Mobley's strategies to finding a job like those that you have found?

OTHER SITES ON GETTING A JOB WITH A SOCIOLOGY DEGREE	
URL LINK	SUMMARY: WHO RUNS THE SITE? DESCRIPTION?

NEW TOPIC:	
URL LINK	SUMMARY: WHO RUNS THE SITE? DESCRIPTION?

NEW TOPIC:	
URL LINK	SUMMARY: WHO RUNS THE SITE? DESCRIPTION?

NEW TOPIC:

URL LINK	SUMMARY: WHO RUNS THE SITE? DESCRIPTION?

NEW TOPIC:

URL LINK	SUMMARY: WHO RUNS THE SITE? DESCRIPTION?

NEW TOPIC:

URL LINK	SUMMARY: WHO RUNS THE SITE? DESCRIPTION?

Research Navigator Guide: Sociology

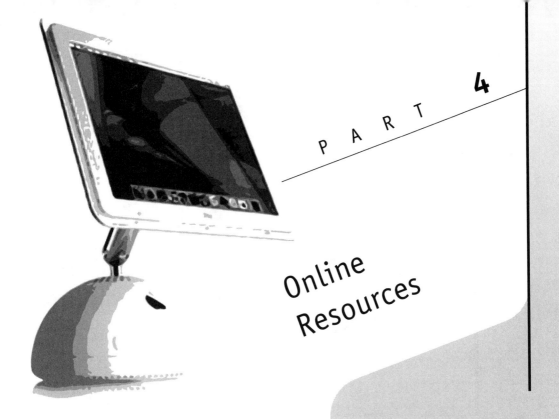

PART 4

Online Resources

Internet Sites Useful in Sociology

URLs frequently change or disappear. If you can't find a site, use one of the search engines listed below to look for it by name.

General Useful Sites

American Studies Web

http://www.georgetown.edu/crossroads/asw

Elwell's Glossary of Sociology

http://campus.murraystate.edu/academic/faculty/
frank.elwell/prob3/GLOSSARY/socgloss.htm

Internet Resources for Sociology Students

http://www.xu.edu/polsci&soc_dept/resources_soc.html

Library of Congress

http://www.loc.gov

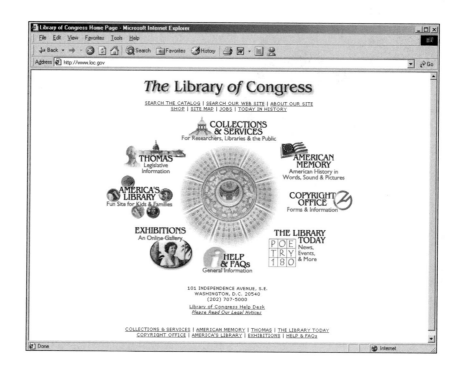

Maricopa

http://www.mcli.dist.maricopa.edu/tl/

SOCNET: Sociology Courses and Curricular Resources

http://www.mcmaster.ca/socscidocs/w3virtsoclib/
socnet.htm

World Lecture Hall

http://www.utexas.edu/world/lecture/

Search Engines

AltaVista Search

http://www.altavista.digital.com

Excite Netsearch

http://www.excite.com

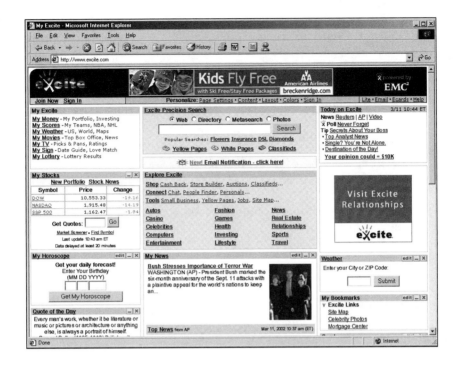

Lycos Search

`http://www.lycos.com`

WebCrawler Search

`http://webcrawler.com`

Yahoo! Search

`http://www.yahoo.com/search.html`

General Sociology Sites

American Sociological Association

`http://www.asanet.org`

BUBL Links: Sociology

`http://link.bubl.ac.uk/sociology`

Research Navigator Guide: Sociology

Clearinghouse: Social Sciences and Social Issues

`http://www.clearinghouse.net/`

Electronic Journal of Sociology

`http://www.sociology.org/`

Galaxy Guide to Sociology

`http://www.einet.net/galaxy/Social-Sciences/`
`Sociology.html`

International Sociological Association

`http://www.ucm.es/info/isa`

Julian Dierkes' Sociology Links at Princeton

`http://www.sociolog.com`

McGraw Hill's Social Science Web Resources

`http://www.mhhe.com/catalogs/hss/sociology`

Social Science Ready Reference

`http://www.mnsfld.edu/depts/lib/mu-scref.html`

Sociological Abstracts Home Page

`http://www.socabs.org`

Sociological Tour of Cyberspace

`http://www.trinity.edu/~mkearl/index.html`

Sociology Courses on the Internet

`http://www.mcmaster.ca/socscidocs/w3virtsoclib/`
`socnet.htm`

Sociology Listservs

`http://www.acs.ryerson.ca/soc/listserv.html`

Sociology Places to Explore

http://hakatai.mcli.dist.maricopa.edu/smc/ml/
sociology.html

Sociology Weblinks at the University of Southern Indiana (USI)

http://www.usi.edu/libarts/socio/sd_wblnk.htm

SocioSite: Sociology in the Netherlands

http://www.pscw.uva.nl/sociosite

SOSIG: Social Science Information Gateway

http://sosig.esrc.bris.ac.uk

Progressive Sociologists Network

http://csf.colorado.edu/psn/

U. C. Berkeley Libraries: Government and Social Science Information

http://www.lib.berkeley.edu/GSSI/sociolog.html

U. Colorado's WWW Resources for Sociologists

http://socsci.colorado.edu/SOC/RES

U. Missouri-St. Louis Sociology Links

http://www.umsl.edu/~sociolog/resource.htm

Western Connecticut State University's Sociology Internet Resources

http://vax.wcsu.edu/socialsci/socres.html

WWW Virtual Library: U.S. Government Information Sources

http://www.nttc.edu/resources/governement/govresource
s.asp

Yahoo!: Sociology

http://www.yahoo.com/Social_Science/Sociology

Aging

The AARP Guide to Internet Resources Related to Aging

http://www.aarp.org/cyber/guide1.htm

Administration on Aging

http://www.aoa.dhhs.gov

Online Periodicals on Aging

http://www.usc.edu/isd/elecresources/subject/
social_Geront.html

AOA Directory of WEB and Gopher Sites on Aging

http://www.aoa.dhhs.gov/aoa/webres/craig.htm

AOA Internet and Email Resources on Aging

http://www.aoa.dhhs.gov/aoa/pages/jpostlst.html

Clifton E. Barber's Internet Information on Aging

http://lamar.colostate.edu/~barberhd/
Internetaginglinks.htm

Institute for Human Development, Life Course and Aging

http://www.utoronto.ca/lifecourse

Geriatrics Links

http://www.medwebplus.com/subject/Geriatrics.html

National Institute on Aging

http://www.nih.gov/nia/

National Council on the Aging

http://www.ncoa.org/

Recent Developments in Age Discrimination Law

http://www.lawinfo.com/forum/age.html

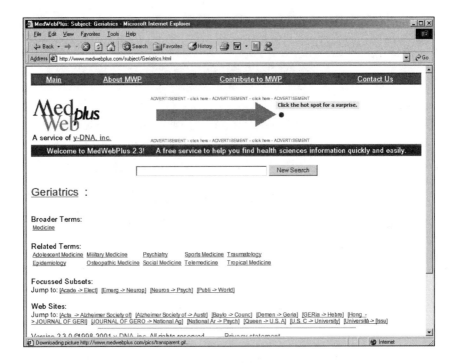

Social Gerontology and the Aging Revolution

`http://WWW.Trinity.Edu/~mkearl/geron.html`

Web Sites on Aging

`http://www.aoa.dhhs.gov/agingsites/default.htm`

Applied Sociology

American Sociological Association Section on Sociological Practice

`http://www.asanet.org/sections/sphome.html`

Evaluation Review: Journal of Applied Social Research

`http://www.sagepub.co.uk/journals/details/j0092.html`

Keith Appleby's Research Resources in Social Science

`http://www.researchresources.net/socio.htm`

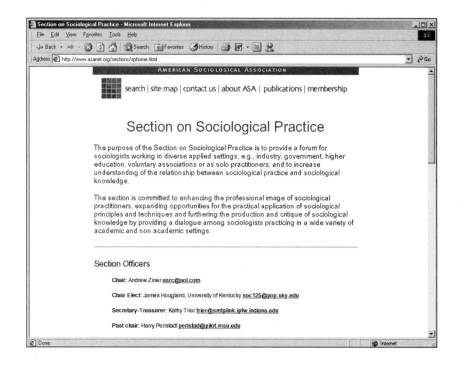

Society for Applied Sociology

http://www.appliedsoc.org/

Sociological Research Online

http://www.socresonline.org.uk/

Applied Tools

American Evaluation Association

http://www.eval.org/index.html

Business Process Reengineering and Innovation

http://www.brint.com/BPR.htm

Creative Problem Solving

http://www.changedynamics.com/samples/probsolv.htm

Creative Problem Solving Templates

http://www.changedynamics.com/samples/samples.htm

Enterprise Reengineering

http://www.reengineering.com/

High Performance Team

http://rampages.onramp.net/~bodwell/home.htm

Social Science Research Methods: Resources for Teachers

http://www.siu.edu/~hawkes/methods.html

Self Directed Work Team (SDWT)

http://users.ids.net/~brim/sdwth.html

Teams and Work Teams

http://www.workteams.unt.edu/

World Future Society

http://www.wfs.org/

Collective Behavior and Social Movements

ASA Section on Collective Behavior and Social Movements

http://www.asanet.org/sections/collect.html

Ex-Cult.org

http://www.ex-cult.org/

Information on Militias (Links)

http://www.well.com/user/srhodes/militia.html

Neo-Militia Links Page

http://www.militia-watchdog.org/m1.htm

Pressure Groups/Interest Groups/Social Movements

http://www.library.ubc.ca/poli/cpwebint.html

Research Navigator Guide: Sociology

Theories of Social Movements and their Current Development in Soviet Society

http://lucy.ukc.ac.uk/csacpub/russian/mamay.html

Activist Groups

Cures Not Wars Online

http://www.cures-not-wars.org

Families Against Mandatory Minimums

http://www.famm.org

Action Groups on the Internet: Community Groups Fighting for Justice

http://www.uaw.org/links/link303x.cfm?sec=4&subsec=10

Institute for Global Communication's Communities of Activists and Organizations

http://www.igc.org/igc

Research Navigator Guide: Sociology

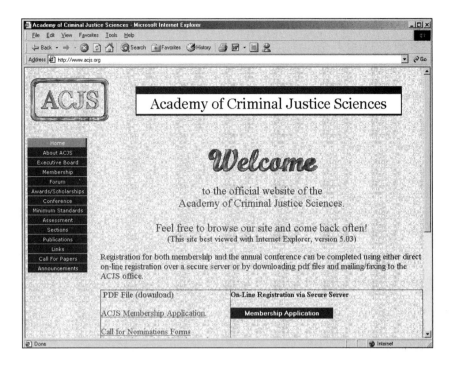

No Compromise's Activist Links

http://www.nocompromise.org/resources/index.html

Criminology, Deviance, and Criminal Justice

Academy of Criminal Justice Sciences

http://www.acjs.org/

Access to Justice Network (Canadian)

http://www.acjnet.org

American Bar Association

http://www.abanet.org

American Correctional Association

http://www.corrections.com/aca/

American Society of Criminology

http://www.asc41.com/

Bureau of Justice Statistics

http://www.ojp.usdoj.gov/bjs

Canadian Centre on Substance Abuse

http://www.ccsa.ca

Court TV Online

http://www.courttv.com

The Critical Criminology Division of the American Society of Criminology

http://www.critcrim.org

Drug Reform Coordination Network

http://www.drcnet.org

International Legal Resource Guide

http://www.ilrg.com

Justice Information Center

http://www.ncjrs.org

Life Education Network: Links on Drugs, Violence and AIDS Prevention

http://www.lec.org

National Institute on Drug Abuse (NIDA)

http://www.nida.nih.gov/NIDAHome.html

National Institute of Justice

http://www.ojp.usdoj.gov/nij/

National Center for Victims of Crime

http://www.ncvc.org

PAVNET: Partners Against Violence Network

www.pavnet.org

Prevention Online (Prevline)

http://www.health.org

United States Parole Commission

http://www.usdoj.gov/uspc/

Yahoo!: Crime

http://www.yahoo.com/society_and_culture/crime

Juvenile Delinquency

Juvenile Justice WWW Sites

http://www.ncjrs.org/jjwww.htm

Office of Juvenile Justice and Delinquency Prevention

http://ojjdp.ncjrs.org/

Resources for Working with At Risk Youth

http://iccs.csumb.edu/html/community/riskyouth/index.html

Vision Quest Program for At-Risk Youth

http://www.vq.com/

Culture

ASA Sociology of Culture Section

http://www.asanet.org/sections/culture.html

Chinese Historical and Cultural Project

http://www.chcp.org

Cultures of the Andes

http://www.andes.org/

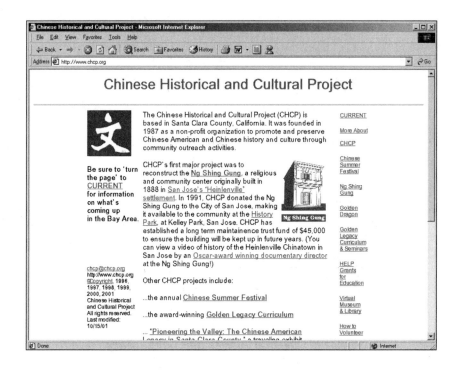

Exploring Ancient World Cultures

http://eawc.evansville.edu/index.htm

French Culture

http://frenchculture.about.com/culture/frenchculture/

The Library of Congress: American Memory

http://rs6.loc.gov

Native American Arts, Humanites and Culture

http://www.tahtonka.com/

NativeWeb: Earth's Indigenous People

www.nativeweb.org

Russian Culture at About.com

http://goeasteurope.about.com/cs/russia

The Ultimate Jewish/Israel Link Launcher

http://ucsu.colorado.edu/~jsu/launcher.html

U. of Oregon Center for Asian and Pacific Studies

http://darkwing.uoregon.edu/~caps

U. of Virginia: The Multicultural Pavilion

http://curry.edschool.virginia.edu/go/multicultural

The Web of Culture

http://www.webofculture.com

Databanks and Providers

Applied Social Data Center Home Page

http://www.cwu.edu/~asdc/home.html

General Social Survey

http://www.icpsr.umich.edu/gss

UCSD Social Sciences Data Collection

http://ssds.ucsd.edu/ssdc/catalog.html

U.S. Statistical Abstract

http://www.census.gov/statab/www

Demography, Population, and Urbanization

American Demographics

http://www.inside.com/default.asp?entity=AmericanDemo

Applied Demography

http://www.prb.org/

Center for Demography and Ecology

http://www.ssc.wisc.edu/cde/

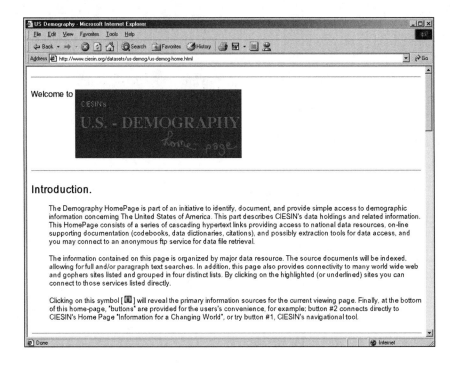

United Nation's Information on Population and Demography

`http://www.library.yale.edu/un/un3b8.htm`

Ciesin's US Demography

`http://www.ciesin.org/datasets/us-demog/`
`us-demog-home.html`

Intentional Communities

`http://www.ic.org`

Manfred Davidmann on Community

`http://www.solbaram.org/indexes/cmmuni.html`

National Civic League

`http://www.ncl.org/`

Pennsylvania State University: Population Research Institute

`http://www.pop.psu.edu`

Research Navigator Guide: Sociology

Princeton University: Office of Population Research Data Archive

http://opr.princeton.edu/archive

Princeton University: Population Index on the Web

http://popindex.princeton.edu

Rural and Small Town Programme

http://www.mta.ca/rstp

Rural Sociological Society

http://ruralsociology.org

Social Science Research Computing Center's Data Library

http://www.spc.uchicago.edu/DATALIB/datalib.cgi?

The Urban Institute

http://www.urban.org

U.S. Census Bureau

http://www.census.gov

U.S. Census Bureau: Census State Data Centers

http://www.census.gov/sdc/www

U.S. Dept. of Housing and Urban Development: Neighborhood Networks

http://www.hud.gov/nnw/nnwindex.html

U.S. Gazetteer

http://www.census.gov/cgi-bin/gazetteer

USA CityLink Home Page

http://usacitylink.com

WWW Virtual Library: Demography & Population Studies

http://demography.anu.edu.au/VirtualLibrary

Economy

ASA Section on Organizations, Occupations, and Work

http://campus.northpark.edu/sociology/oow

Bureau of Labor Statistics

http://www.bls.gov/home.htm

Electronic Policy Network

http://www.epn.org

Institute of Industrial Relations

http://violet.berkeley.edu/~iir

Job Accommodation Network

http://janweb.icdi.wvu.edu

LaborNet

http://www.labornet.org

Legal Information Institute: Employment Discrimination Law Materials

http://www.law.cornell.edu/topics/
employment_discrimination.html

Manfred Davidmann on Economics

http://www.solbaram.org/indexes/ecnmcs.html

United Mine Workers of America

http://www.umwa.org/homepage.shtml

The Urban Institute: Widening Wage Inequality

http://www.urban.org/periodcl/prr25_1b.htm

U.S. Dept. of Agriculture: Economic Research Service

http://www.ers.usda.gov

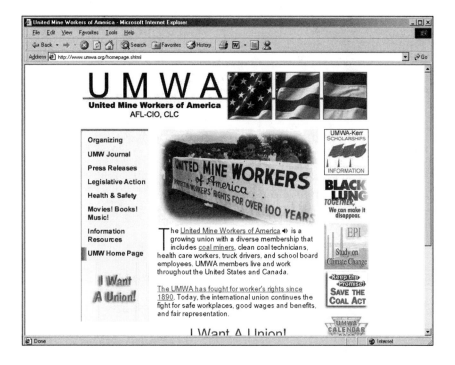

Education

American Association of Community Colleges

http://www.aacc.nche.edu

Ask ERIC Education Information

http://ericir.syr.edu

Aspen Institute

http://www.aspeninst.org/

EduCause: Managing and Using Information Resources in Higher Education

http://cause-www.colorado.edu

The Center for Education Reform

http://edreform.com

Research Navigator Guide: Sociology

Commonwealth of Learning

http://www.col.org

Council of the Great City Schools

http://www.cgcs.org

Diversity University (MOO provider)

http://www.du.org

Education World

http://www.education-world.com/

ERIC: Urban Education Web

http://eric-web.tc.columbia.edu

Galaxy Social Science Education Resources

http://galaxy.einet.net/galaxy/Social-Sciences.html

Global Network Academy

http://www.gnacademy.org

National Education Association (NEA)

http://www.nea.org/

School District Data Book Profiles: 1989–1990

http://govinfo.kerr.orst.edu/sddb-stateis.html

School District Demographics

http://proximityone.com/plsd.htm

U.S. Department of Education

http://www.ed.gov

U.S. Department of Education: Online Resources

http://www.ed.gov/about/organizations.jsp

Yahoo!: Education

http://www.yahoo.com/Education

Environment

The British Columbia Ministry of Water, Land, and Air Protection

http://www.gov.bc.ca/wlap

Centre for Economic and Social Studies on the Environment

http://www.ulb.ac.be:80/ceese

Ecological Society of America

http://www.sdsc.edu/ESA/ESA.htm

EcoNet

http://www.igc.org/igc/econet/index.html

EcoTrust

http://www.ecotrust.org

EnviroLink

http://envirolink.netforchange.com/

Government Information Sharing Project

http://govinfo.kerr.orst.edu

Linkages: Resources for Environment and Development Policy Makers

http://www.iisd.ca/

National Environmental Trust

http://www.environet.org

National Library for the Environment

http://www.cnie.org/nle/

Research Navigator Guide: Sociology

Research Navigator Guide: Sociology

Renewable Energy Policy Project & Center for Renewable Energy and Sustainable Technology (REPP-CREST)

http://www.crest.org

Student Environmental Action Coalition

http://www.seac.org

The Water Environment Federation

http://www.wef.org/

Yahoo!: Environment and Nature Organizations

http://www.yahoo.com/Society_and_Culture/
Environment_and_Nature/Organizations

Yahoo!: Pollution Activist Groups

http://www.yahoo.com/Society_and_Culture/
Environment_and_Nature/Pollution/Activist_Groups

Ethics

Applied Ethics Resources on WWW

http://www.ethics.ubc.ca/papers/AppliedEthics.html

Institute for Global Ethics

http://www.globalethics.org/

Family

DHHS Administration for Children and Families

http://www.acf.dhhs.gov

Family.com Home Page

http://family.go.com/

The Family Research Council

http://www.frc.org

Family Village Library

http://www.familyvillage.wisc.edu/library.htm

Ring of Single Parents

http://c.webring.com/hub?ring=sfvoices

U. of Colorado's Family Sociology Resources

http://osiris.colorado.edu/SOC/RES/family.html

Gender

Above & Beyond's Gender Resources Newsletters

http://www.abgender.com/news/index.shtml

American Association of University Women

http://www.aauw.org/4000/extlinks.html

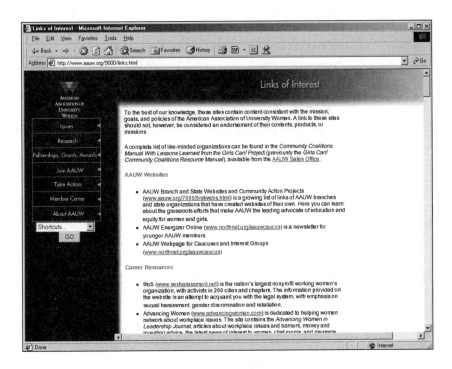

Feminist Activist Resources on the Net

http://www.igc.apc.org/women/feminist.html

Feminist.Com: Resources and Links

http://www.feminist.com/resources/links

The Feminist Majority: Internet Gateway

http://www.feminist.org/gateway/1_gatway.html

Feminists for Free Expression

http://www.ffeusa.org

Gay and Lesbian Alliance Against Defamation

http://www.glaad.org/

Gender and the Law at the University of Dayton

http://www.udayton.edu/~gender/

Gender and Sexuality Links

http://eserver.org/gender

Gender-Related Electronic Forums

http://www-unix.umbc.edu/~korenman/wmst/forums.html

Ingersoll Gender Center

http://www.ingersollcenter.org/

National Gay & Lesbian Task Force Links

http://www.ngltf.org/about/links.cfm

National Organization of Women: Resources on the Internet

http://www.now.org/resource.html

Voice of the Shuttle: Gender Studies Page

http://vos.ucsb.edu/browse.asp?id=2711

Women and Gender Studies Links at Louisiana State University (LSU)

http://www.artsci.lsu.edu/wgs/links/links.html

WomensNet

http://www.voiceofwomen.com/other.html

Women's Studies/Women's Issues Resource Sites

http://www-unix.umbc.edu/~korenman/wmst/links.html

WWWomen! Search Directory for Women Online

http://www.wwwomen.com

WWW Virtual Library: Men's Issues Page

http://www.vix.com/pub/men/index.html

WWW Virtual Library: Men's Movement Organizations

http://www.vix.com/pub/men/orgs/orgs.html

Yahoo!: Gender

http://www.yahoo.com/Society_and_Culture/Gender

Medicine and Health

AIDS Treatment News Archive

http://www.immunet.org/atn

American Cancer Society: Cancer Reference Information

http://www.cancer.org/eprise/main/docroot/CRI/cri_0

ASH Links to Smoking Related Sites

http://ash.org/otherweb/index.html

Centers for Disease Control & Prevention

http://www.cdc.gov

Department of Health and Human Services

http://www.os.dhhs.gov

HealthLinks

http://healthlinks.washington.edu

Medicine and Health Sources at Bridgewater State University

http://www.bridgew.edu/DEPTS/MAXWELL/medicine.htm

Medicine Online: Medical Related Sites

http://www.mol.net

University of Texas' Medicine and Health Resources Page

http://biotech.icmb.utexas.edu/pages/science/
health.html

World Health Organization

http://www.who.ch

Yahoo!: Health

http://www.yahoo.com/Health

Media

Computer Mediated Communication Magazine Index

http://www.december.com/cmc/mag

Just Think Foundation: Links to Think

http://www.justthink.org/outsideresources.html

Mass Media and Culture Resources

http://www.uark.edu/~aca/studies/mediaculture.html

The Media History Project

http://mediahistory.umn.edu

Freedom Forum

http://www.freedomforum.org/

Project Censored: News That Didn't Make the News

http://www.projectcensored.org/frontpagenews/7_16_00p
eter.html

Visionary Media

http://www.visionarymedia.com/

Yahoo!: News and Media

http://www.yahoo.com/News_and_Media

News Media Online

CNN Digest

http://cnn.com/DIGEST

Jerusalem Post

http://www.jpost.co.il

Mojo Wire (Mother Jones Interactive)

http://www.mojones.com

National Public Radio Online

http://www.npr.org

Newspapers On Line

http://ftp.sff.net/people/jack.haldeman/papers.htm

NY Times Fax (subscription needed)

http://nytimesfax.com

Public Broadcasting System (PBS) Online

http://www.pbs.org

Seattle Times

http://www.seatimes.com

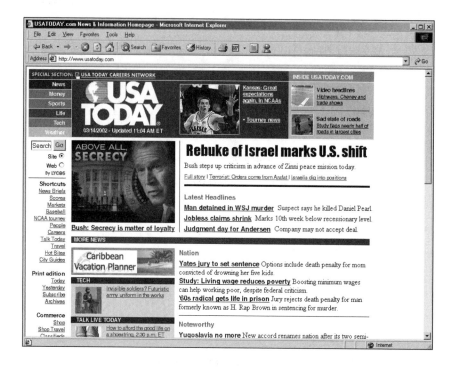

The Times and The Sunday Times

http://www.the-times.co.uk/news/pages/
home.html?000999

USA Today

http://www.usatoday.com

Politics

African National Congress Home Page

http://www.anc.org.za

Congressional Quarterly

http://www.cq.com/

Consumer Information Center

http://pueblo.gsa.gov

C-SPAN

http://www.c-span.org

Electronic Policy Network

http://epn.org/

League of Women Voters

http://www.lwv.org/

National Political Index

http://www.politicalindex.com

The Organization of American States

http://www.oas.org

Political Resources on the Net

http://www.politicalresources.net

Politics1

http://www.politics1.com/

Project Vote Smart

http://www.vote-smart.org

Virtual Tour of the U.S. Government

http://www.virtualfreesites.com/us-gov.html

Yahoo!: Politics

http://www.yahoo.com/Government/Politics

Poverty and Homelessness

HomeAid America: Building Hope and Homes for the Temporarily Homeless

http://www.HomeAid.org/index1.html

HungerWeb: Researchers Entry Point

http://www.brown.edu/Departments/World_Hunger_Program
/hungerweb/researchers.html

Institute for Research on Poverty

http://www.ssc.wisc.edu/irp

International Homeless Discussion List & Archives

http://csf.colorado.edu/homeless/index.html

Joint Center for Poverty Research

http://www.jcpr.org/about.html

Michigan Program on Poverty and Social Welfare Policy

http://www.ssw.umich.edu/poverty/mission.html

National Center for Children in Poverty

http://cpmcnet.columbia.edu/dept/nccp

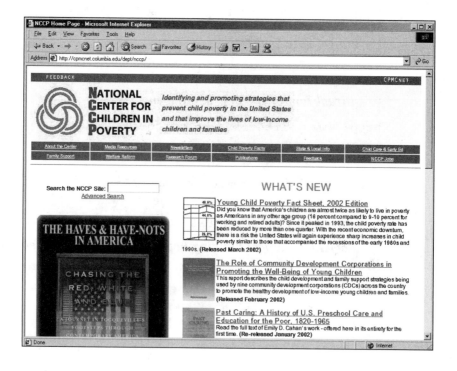

National Coalition for the Homeless Directories

http://nch.ari.net/direct1.html

National Coalition for the Homeless Online Library

http://nch.ari.net/database.html

National Law Center on Homelessness and Poverty

http://www.nlchp.org/

Resources for Ending Poverty and Hunger

http://www.resultsusa.org

Twentieth Century Fund Brief on Welfare Reform

http://www.tcf.org/Publications/Basics/welfare/
Introduction.html

UMCOR Hunger/Poverty Ministries

http://gbgm-umc.org/umcor/hunger.stm

UN ReliefWeb: Related Sites List

http://www.reliefweb.int/contacts/related.html

U.S. Census Bureau: Poverty 2000

http://www.census.gov/hhcs/www/poverty00.html

U.S. DHHS: Federal Poverty Guidelines and Measurement

http://aspe.os.dhhs.gov/poverty/poverty.htm

Yahoo!: Welfare Reform

http://dir.yahoo.com/Society_and_Culture/
Issues_and_Causes/Poverty/Welfare/Reform

Race and Ethnicity

Carnegie Mellon Race Links

http://eng.hss.cmu.edu/race

Cultural Survival

http://www.cs.org/

European Research Centre on Migration and Ethnic Relations

http://www.ercomer.org

Ethics Updates Page on Race, Multiculturalism and Ethnicity

http://ethics.acusd.edu/Applied/race/race.html

The Final Call: Black Community Issues and Events

http://www.finalcall.com

General Race & Ethnicity Resources—American Studies Web

http://cfdev.georgetown.edu/cndls/asw/aswsub.cfm?head
1=Race%2C%20Ethnicity%2C%20and%20Identity

Legal Information Institute: Civil Rights and Discrimination

http://fatty.law.cornell.edu/topics/civil_rights.html

National Civil Rights Museum

http://www.civilrightsmuseum.org

Race and Ethnicity Online

http://www.providence.edu/polisci/rep/

Texas A&M Race and Ethnic Studies Institute

http://resi.tamu.edu/index.html

Trinity Sociology: Race and Ethnicity

http://WWW.Trinity.Edu/~mkearl/race.html

Voice of the Shuttle: Minority Studies Page

http://vos.ucsb.edu/browse.asp?id=2721

WWW Virtual Library: Migration and Ethnic Relations

http://www.ercomer.org/wwwvl/

Yahoo!: Migration and Ethnic Relations

```
http://www.yahoo.com/Social_Science/
Migration_and_Ethnic_Relations
```

Yahoo!: Race and Racism

```
http://dir.yahoo.com/Society_and_Culture/
Issues_and_Causes/Race_and_Racism
```

Religion

American Academy of Religion

```
http://www.aar-site.org/
```

The Center for Reformed Theology and Apologetics

```
http://www.reformed.org/
```

Comparative Religion Resources

```
http://www.lib.washington.edu/subject/CompReligion/
```

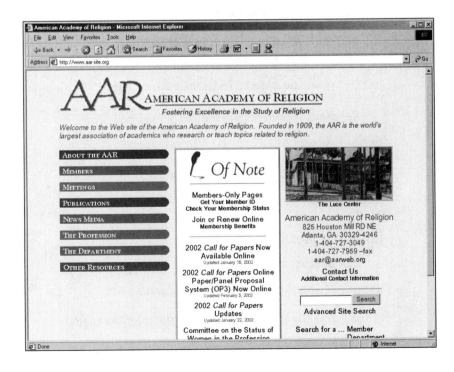

Cult Awareness & Information Centre—Australia

http://student.uq.edu.au/~py101663/zentry1.htm

Fighting the Radical Religious Right (useful links)

http://ftp.qrd.org/qrd/www/rrr/rrrpage.html

General Theory of Religion

http://world.std.com/~awolpert

Index of Religious Links

http://www.religioustolerance.org/toc.htm

Judaism and Jewish Resources

http://shamash.org/trb/judaism.html

New Religious Movements: Web Sites

http://www.gtu.edu/library/LibraryNRMLinks.html

Ontario Consultants on Religious Tolerance

http://www.religioustolerance.org

Religious Movements & Alternative Spirituality, An Annotated Directory of Internet Resources

http://www.academicinfo.net/nrms.html

Religious Resources on the Net

http://www.religiousresources.org

Religious Studies Electronic Library

http://library.uwaterloo.ca/discipline/religious/

Research Methods

ASA Section on Methods

http://lion.icpsr.umich.edu/methsect

Bill Trochim's Center for Social Research Methods

http://trochim.human.cornell.edu/

The Foundation Center (grants)

http://fdncenter.org

Glossary of Social Science Computing and Social Science Data Terms

http://odwin.ucsd.edu/glossary

PARnet: The Cornell Participatory Action Research Network

http://www.parnet.org

The Qualitative Report

http://www.nova.edu/ssss/QR/index.html

Research Engines for the Social Sciences

http://www.carleton.ca/~cmckie/research.html

Research Methods

http://www.siu.edu/~hawkes/methods.html

Research Resources for the Social Sciences

http://www.socsciresearch.com

Sociological Research Online

http://www.soc.surrey.ac.uk/socresonline

Statistics

Fedstats: One Stop Shopping for Federal Statistics

http://www.fedstats.gov/

SPSS Inc.

http://www.spss.com

Statistical Resources on the Web: Sociology

http://www.lib.umich.edu/govdocs/stsoc.html

Research Navigator Guide: Sociology

Social Change

Data Center: A Resource for Progressive Social Change

http://www.igc.org/datacenter/

DOE's Center of Excellence for Sustainable Development

http://www.sustainable.doe.gov

Ed Brown's Resource Information: Global Change

http://www.stile.lut.ac.uk/~gyedb/STILE/t0000459.html

Good Works: A National Directory of Social Change Organizations

http://www.essential.org/goodworks/

Internet Resources on Sustainability

http://www.chebucto.ns.ca/Environment/SCN/
CommLink/SCN-netguide.html

Longwave and Social Cycles Resource Centre

http://www.1-888.com/longwave/index.html

Peace Brigades International

http://www.igc.apc.org/pbi

Peace Brigades International: Web Links

http://www.igc.apc.org/pbi/links.html

Social Change—A Collection of Relevant Book Chapters

http://www.spc.uchicago.edu/ssr1/PRELIMS/change.html

Soros Foundation Network for Open Society

http://www.soros.org

Social Psychology

ASA Social Psychology Section

http://www.asanet.org/sections/socpsych.html

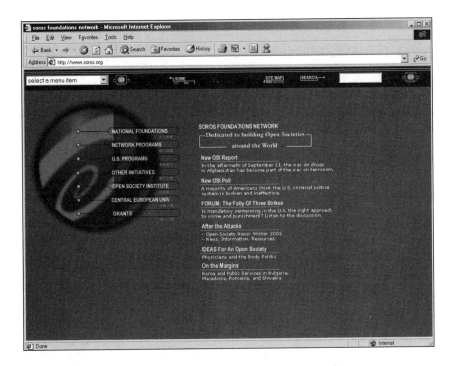

The British Journal of Social Psychology

http://www.bps.org.uk/publications/jSP_1.cfm

Current Research in Social Psychology

http://www.uiowa.edu/~grpproc/crisp/crisp.html

George's Page (George Herbert Mead)

http://paradigm.soci.brocku.ca:80/~lward

Psychology Centre: Social and Cultural Psychology

http://server.bmod.athabascau.ca/html/aupr/social.htm

Social Psychology Network

http://www.socialpsychology.org/

Social Psychology Resources at Haverford College

http://www.haverford.edu/psych/SocPsycpage.html

Society for Personality and Social Psychology

http://www.spsp.org/

A Sociological Social Psychology

http://www.trinity.edu/~mkearl/socpsy.html

SOSIG–World–Social Psychology

http://www.sosig.ac.uk/roads/subject-listing/World-cat/socpsych.htm

Social Stratification

Albert Benschop's Alphabetical Bibliography on Class

http://www.pscw.uva.nl/sociosite/CLASS/bibA.html

International Stratification and Mobility File

http://www.fss.uu.nl/soc/hg/ismf/index.htm

Stratification and Society

http://www.digeratiweb.com/sociorealm

What Is Social Stratification?

http://www.sdsmt.edu/online-courses/is/soc100/soc_strat.htm

Social Structure and Social Interaction

Alliance for Redesigning Government

http://www.alliance.napawash.org/

Ed Brown's Political Economy Archive

http://www.stile.lut.ac.uk/~gyedb/STILE/index.html

Ed Brown's Resource Information: Capitalism

http://www.stile.lut.ac.uk/~gyedb/STILE/t0000460.html

Ed Brown's Resource Information: Development Theory

http://www.stile.lut.ac.uk/~gyedb/STILE/t0000425.html

Ed Brown's Resource Information; Neo-marxism

http://www.stile.lut.ac.uk/~gyedb/STILE/t0000455.html

A Gallery of Social Structures: Network Visualization

http://www.mpi-fg-koeln.mpg.de:80/~lk/netvis.html

Max Planck Institute for the Study of Societies

http://www.mpi-fg-koeln.mpg.de

WSN: The World-Systems Conferencing Electronic Network

http://csf.Colorado.EDU/wsystems

Sociological Theory

"An Outline of the Social System"

http://www.spc.uchicago.edu/ssr1/PRELIMS/
Theory/parsons.html

ASA Section on Marxist Sociology

http://csf.colorado.edu/psn/marxist-sociology/
index.html

Association for Humanist Sociology

http://www.humanistsoc.org

Critical Theory-Driven Inquiry

http://www2.uchicago.edu/jnl-crit-inq

CTHEORY

http://www.ctheory.com/

The Marx/Engels Internet Archive

http://csf.Colorado.edu/psn/marx

Marx and Engels' Writings

http://english-www.hss.cmu.edu/marx

Norbert Elias and Process Sociology

http://www.usyd.edu.au/su/social/elias/elias.html

Postmodern Culture

http://jefferson.village.virginia.edu/pmc/
contents.all.html

Postmodern Thought Links at the University of Colorado, Denver

http://carbon.cudenver.edu/~mryder/itc_data/
postmodern.html

Society for the Study of Symbolic Interaction

http://sun.soci.niu.edu/~sssi

Sociology Links from Patrick Macartney

http://www.angelfire.com/ma/Socialworld/
Sociology.html

Spoon Collective for Discussion of Philosophical Issues

http://jefferson.village.virginia.edu/~spoons

Tocqueville's Democracy in America

http://xroads.virginia.edu/~HYPER/DETOC/home.html

The Works of John Locke

http://libertyonline.hypermall.com/Locke/Default.htm

Technology and Computers

Alliance for Public Technology

http://apt.org/index.html

ASA Section on Sociology and Computers

http://www.asanet.org/sections/computer.html

Association for Computing Machinery

http://www.acm.org/

Association for Progressive Communications

http://www.apc.org

The Center for Democracy and Technology

http://www.cdt.org/

Computer Professionals for Social Responsibility

http://www.cpsr.org/

CTHEORY: Journal of Theory, Technology and Culture

http://www.ctheory.com

Scientists for Global Responsibility

http://www.gn.apc.org/sgr

Society for the Social Studies of Science

http://www.lsu.edu:80/guests/ssss/public_html

Street-Level Youth Media: Communications Technology for Youth

http://www.iit.edu/~livewire

Violence and Abuse

BC Institute Against Family Violence

http://www.bcifv.org/

ConflictNet: Conflict Resolution Resources

http://www.igc.org/igc/gateway/pnindex.html

Domestic Violence Pages

http://www.athens.net/~rblum/dvpindex.html

Kate Orman's Violence Against Women Page

http://www.zip.com.au/~korman/dv

Links on Violence and Abuse, Q Web Sweden

http://www.qweb.kvinnoforum.se/violence/index.html

MINCAVA: Minnesota Center Against Violence and Abuse

http://www.mincava.umn.edu

National Network for Child Care: Child Abuse Links

http://www.nncc.org/Abuse/abuse.links.html

New York City Multidisciplinary Child Fatality Review

http://www.sunlink.net/~browning/index.htm#home

Nonviolence International

http://www.members.tripod.com/nviusa

SafetyNet Domestic Violence Resources

http://www.cybergrrl.com/dv.html

Yahoo!: Domestic Violence Organizations

http://www.yahoo.com/Society_and_Culture/Crime/
Types_of_Crime/Domestic_Violence/Organizations

Other Online Resources

Allyn & Bacon Social Problems Supersite

http://www.ablongman.com/socprobs
The Social Problems Supersite is organized around 14 core social problems topics. The *Where Do You Stand?* Feature offers a series of survey questions designed to prepare students for the various issues within each social problem area. Other features include an online glossary, interactive study guide (with multiple choice, true/false, fill-in-the-blank, and essay questions), internet resources, message board, and critical thinking questions.

Companion Web Sites

http://www.abinteractive.com/gallery
Our Companion Web sites use the Internet to provide you with various opportunities for further study and exploration. The CW offers study content and activities related to the text, as well as an interactive, online study guide. Quizzes containing multiple choice, true/false, and essay questions can be graded instantly, and forwarded to your instructor for recording—all online. For a complete list of titles with a CW, visit **www.abinteractive. com/gallery.**

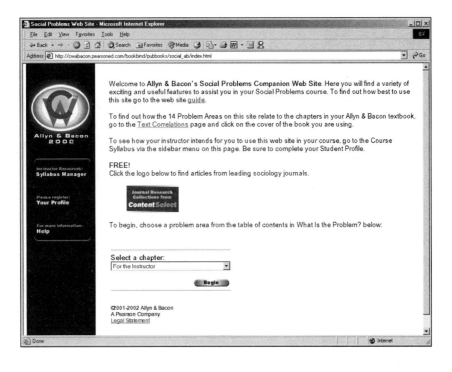

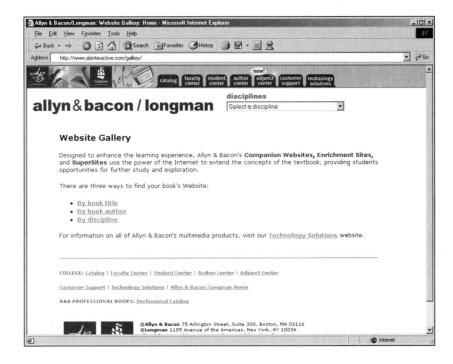

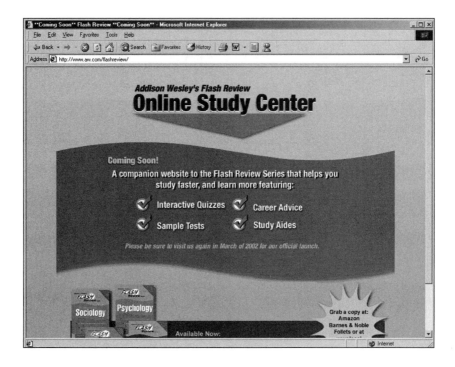

Flash Review Series for Introduction to Sociology

`http://www.flashreview.com`

This is the companion Web site to the Flash Review for Introduction to Sociology, a new kind of study guide that features interactive quizzes, career advice, sample tests, and study aides. You can find a copy of the study guide at your local bookseller.

Research Navigator Guide: Sociology

Glossary

Your Own Private Glossary

The Glossary in this book contains reference terms you'll find useful as you get started on the Internet. After a while, however, you'll find yourself running across abbreviations, acronyms, and buzzwords whose definitions will make more sense to you once you're no longer a novice (or "newbie"). That's the time to build a glossary of your own. For now, the Webopedia gives you a place to start.

alias   A simple email address that can be used in place of a more complex one.

AVI   Audio Video Interleave. A video compression standard developed for use with Microsoft Windows. Video clips on the World Wide Web are usually available in both AVI and QuickTime formats.

bandwidth   Internet parlance for capacity to carry or transfer information such as email and Web pages.

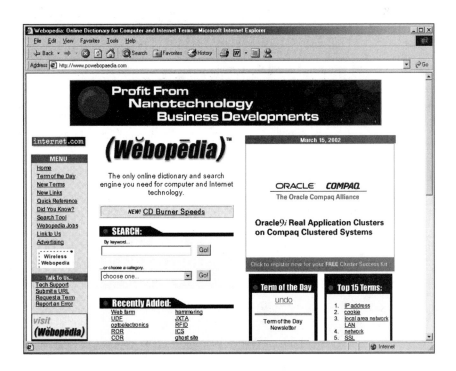

browser   The computer program that lets you view the contents of Web sites.

client   A program that runs on your personal computer and supplies you with Internet services, such as getting your mail.

cyberspace   The whole universe of information that is available from computer networks. The term was coined by science fiction writer William Gibson in his novel *Neuromancer,* published in 1984.

DNS   See *domain name server.*

domain   A group of computers administered as a single unit, typically belonging to a single organization such as a university or corporation.

domain name   A name that identifies one or more computers belonging to a single domain. For example, "apple.com".

domain name server   A computer that converts domain names into the numeric addresses used on the Internet.

download   Copying a file from another computer to your computer over the Internet.

email   Electronic mail.

emoticon   A guide to the writer's feelings, represented by typed characters, such as the Smiley :-). Helps readers understand the emotions underlying a written message.

FAQs   Frequently Asked Questions

flame   A rude or derogatory message directed as a personal attack against an individual or group.

flame war   An exchange of flames (see above).

ftp   File Transfer Protocol, a method of moving files from one computer to another over the Internet.

home page   A page on the World Wide Web that acts as a starting point for information about a person or organization.

hypertext   Text that contains embedded *links* to other pages of text. Hypertext enables the reader to navigate between pages of related information by following links in the text.

LAN   Local Area Network. A computer network that is located in a concentrated area, such as offices within a building.

link   A reference to a location on the Web that is embedded in the text of the Web page. Links are usually highlighted with a different color or underlined to make them easily visible.

listserv   Strictly speaking, a computer program that administers electronic mailing lists, but also used to denote such lists or discussion groups, as in "the writer's listserv."

lurker   A passive reader of an Internet *newsgroup* or *listserv*. A lurker reads messages, but does not participate in the discussion by posting or responding to messages.

mailing list   A subject-specific automated email system. Users subscribe and receive email from other users about the subject of the list.

modem   A device for connecting two computers over a telephone line.

newbie   A new user of the Internet.

newsgroup   A discussion forum in which all participants can read all messages and public replies between the participants.

plug-in   A third-party software program that will lend a Web browser (Netscape, Internet Explorer, etc.) additional features.

quoted   Text in an email message or newsgroup posting that has been set off by the use of vertical bars or > characters in the left-hand margin.

search engine   A computer program that will locate Web sites or files based on specified criteria.

secure   A Web page whose contents are encrypted when sending or receiving information.

server   A computer program that moves information on request, such as a Web server that sends pages to your browser.

Smiley   See *emoticon.*

snail mail   Mail sent the old fashioned way: Write a letter, put it in an envelope, stick on a stamp, and drop it in the mailbox.

spam   Spam is to the Internet as unsolicited junk mail is to the postal system.

URL   Uniform Resource Locator: The notation for specifying addresses on the World Wide Web (e.g. http://www.abacon.com or ftp://ftp.abacon.com).

Usenet   The section of the Internet devoted to *newsgroups.*

Web browser   A program used to navigate and access information on the World Wide Web. Web browsers convert html coding into a display of pictures, sound, and words.

Web page   All the text, graphics, pictures, and so forth, denoted by a single URL beginning with the identifier "http://".

Web site   A collection of World Wide Web pages, usually consisting of a home page and several other linked pages.

Research Navigator Guide: Sociology